Recalibrating
the Labor Market

-or-

*How to have your cake
and time to eat it too*

JOHN CREA

DEDICATION

To Susan, the love of my life.

CONTENTS

PREFACE

I had the good fortune to be on a Danube River cruise a few years back when I came across a construction worksite in Bratislava, Slovakia. There was such a long, scary-looking ladder, I had to snap a picture.

This is not a great photo – it has little artistic merit. It would've been much more interesting if the crew of workers was present, maybe with one guy halfway up the ladder schlepping a 60# bag of cement over his shoulder. I kept the photo anyway and pasted it on my computer desktop to remind myself just why I was writing this book.

The book is about the labor market, about both employers and employees. But the book is decidedly <u>for</u> the workers. For the workers on this construction crew. For the workers in the McDonald's and the coffee shop below. It is for all those who climb ladders at work – be they construction or corporate.

Thank you for taking time to climb off the ladder and read my work.

ACKNOWLEDGMENTS

John Wayne Barker, Mike Greenbaum, and Pat Hanson for their guidance
working with adults with disabilities.
Bob Bertoni for his first-hand knowledge of working on Wall Street.
Rick Bishop for the editing and encouragement along the way.
John Blomquist for pertinent information on piece-rate bonuses at
Andersen Windows and all the material related to "a fair day's work".
Michael and Beverly Cotter for sharing all the valuable material on farming
in the 1930's, and Sue Doocy from the Mower County Historical Society
for putting me in touch with the Cotters.
Barbara Flanagan for the breakdown of 3M's US/OUS business.
Tim Johnson for background on manufacturing strategies at multi-national
corporations.
Louis Johnston for an estimate of the inflationary impact of a shorter
workweek coupled with no drop in salaries.
Rainer Link for the gifts of Piketty and Pinker, and for invaluable feedback
on my writing.
Greg Swanson for the way jobs of administrative workers have changed.
Mike Weber for changes in R&D instrumentation and methodology over
the years.
And all friends and family members who encouraged my efforts.

PHOTO CREDITS

Sonia Bal and her coworkers at Unifiller Systems in Vancouver for the great
photo on the cover!
Michael Cotter and Sue Doocy for photos in the Agriculture section.

Introduction

LET YOUR IMAGINATION run wild for a minute: Picture yourself waving a magic wand and instantly adding 16 hours of free time to your week. 16 hours! Is there anyone who wouldn't take advantage of this magical sleight-of-hand?

All of us who work for a living certainly would because there is never enough time to get everything done at home. That is true no matter what kind of work you do, white collar or blue collar. It is true if you are male or female, rich or poor, urban or rural. It is especially true if you are a parent and a caregiver – juggling schedules at home to check in on grandma, throwing in a load of wash, helping the kids with their homework, making supper and finding time to sit down with everyone to eat, dashing from soccer game to piano lesson to boy scout meeting, getting all the kids back home and settled in for the night, paying any attention at all to your spouse, and somehow getting in a good night's sleep. Never enough hours.

While I don't believe in magic wands any more than I believe in unicorns, I do believe in the power of logical reasoning. And I believe that if we set our minds to it, we can change our lives and become less consumed by our culture of paid work.

It is time to **recalibrate the labor market**, dropping the standard fulltime workweek from 40-hours to something closer to 24-hours. That belief is based on these core convictions:

1. Work is important to all of us; therefore, it is important for all of us to have the chance to work.

   While that sounds trite on the surface, the reader should understand that the meaning of work goes well beyond just 'making a living'. Human beings are social animals who live together in cooperative communities. It is through work that we establish our role in the community, and it is through work that we contribute to society. The compensation we receive for paid employment is simply one measure of our value to the community.

2. Oftentimes, there are not enough jobs to go around.

   Advances in technology and automation make each generation of workers more productive than the last, yet each generation stubbornly sticks to the 40-hour workweek. This frequently leaves us with more people seeking paid employment than there are jobs available.

3. We have a seriously imbalanced labor market.

   The combination of increased productivity with no corresponding decrease in the number of hours worked results in almost regular bouts of high unemployment. This creates a mindset in the labor market where employers hold an unfair advantage over employees when it comes to hiring and compensation decisions.

There is a solution to this dilemma that doesn't call for a mythical magical wand. Just a little common sense.

WE NEED TO GO BACK and look at how we ended up in this situation in the first place. The forty-hour workweek was established eighty years ago, during the great depression, with the enactment of the Fair Labor Standards Act in 1938.* This move to limit the length of the workweek was based on fairness, and was an antidote to the severe unemployment that was manifest in America and around the globe. The idea was very simple. With only so much work to go around, the shorter workweek would force employers to hire a greater number of workers to run their factories and their shops.

This had a profound impact on the labor market. Forty hours a week became the normal fulltime job, and Monday through Friday the normal workweek. This standard became culturally ingrained, not just in America, but across the industrialized world.

AS IT TURNS OUT, we've seen just a few changes in the workplace since the 1930's:

80 years ago	Today
Some farmers were still using horses to plow their fields, and all the cows were milked by hand.	Farmers employ 200 HP tractors to plow their fields, and milking a cow by hand is considered a quaint activity reserved for county fairs.

---

* The FLSA essentially ruled that if you are paid hourly, and you put in more than 40 hours in a week, you get time-and-a-half for the overtime worked.

80 years ago	Today
Factories were grimy places filled with thousands of lunchbox-toting production workers who were forced to keep up with the assembly line. They hammered away at repetitive tasks all day long, feeding parts into noisy machines. The factory workers themselves were essentially replaceable cogs in a giant production machine.	Factories are spic-and-span facilities filled with automated machines and robots. There are a handful of humans around, but they are no longer mere extensions of the machines. Production workers are now highly skilled technicians who schedule runs, program the machines, optimize productivity and ensure QC.
An office of any size had a receptionist who answered the phone and greeted guests. There were secretaries, bookkeepers, clerical workers, and managers. Secretaries took dictation using shorthand and translated that cryptic scrawl into legible documents using typewriters and carbon paper. Bookkeepers with green eyeshades manually filled in ledger books with credits and debits. Documents were stored in miles of filing cabinets, and retrieving an old record was a physical activity that took a clerk into a remote file room.	The receptionist is long gone from the front of the office. The remaining workers have jobs that are much more integrated, vertically and horizontally. They are called analysts or coordinators or customer service reps who strive for titles like supervisor or manager or director. There is a personal computer on every desk, and each office worker is capable of being many, many times more productive than their previous selves. (Except perhaps when it comes to retrieving an old record – now hopelessly lost in someone's mislabeled file folder.)

80 years ago	Today
We routinely worked 40 hours per week.	We routinely work 40 hours per week (many of us much more!).

<u>None</u> **of the benefits of increased productivity and labor-saving devices have translated into any free-time for the workers.**

THERE HAVE BEEN some solid efforts to reduce the workweek (e.g. the 30-hour workweek at Kellogg's). Back in the 1930's, John Maynard Keynes predicted that we'd all be working 15 hours a week by the year 2030, and that after putting in a three-hour workday we could turn our thoughts to **more important tasks** of art, culture, and religion. Keynes and others believed there were philosophical and cultural reasons to strive for a shorter workweek that went well beyond the primary economic intent to maintain full employment. (I strongly agree with that sentiment.)

Economists of the day (the 1930's) recognized that technological advances in factories had produced huge productivity gains, and that these were bound to accelerate in the future. Therefore, it was inevitable that the standard workweek would shorten substantially.

But it didn't happen. Once the 40-hour week was effectively codified by the FLSA, it became more than the law of the land. It became culturally established, and was then steadfastly retained by both unions and corporations.

When WWII came around, any thoughts of a shorter workweek were quickly forgotten. The demand for goods to support the war effort skyrocketed, and while working-age men rushed off to join the military, Rosie the Riveter was enlisted to fill in gaps in the workforce.

Following the war, there was an immediate need for reconstruction in Europe and Asia to repair damage wrought by the war. Here at home, there was pent up demand to meet the needs for housing, autos, and such for the returning soldiers and their new spouses as they went about creating the baby boom. The soldiers went back to work in factories and offices, and Rosie went home to raise the kids. The economy kept humming and the overall demand for manufactured goods remained high.

But baby booms don't last forever, and this one petered out around 1965. About that time, Rosie remembered that there were parts of going to work that she liked. She liked getting out of the house. She liked the social connections. She liked having an opportunity to prove herself professionally. She liked getting her own paycheck

With the slowing economy and with the influx of millions of women in the workforce, we might've expected unemployment to really skyrocket in the late 1960's. However, the Vietnam War gave the economy a boost, as did spending on the cold war. And more than anything else, the boys on Madison Avenue had mastered the art of advertising, and we became a <u>very</u> materialistic society with consumers keeping the demand strong for just about everything new under the sun.

The oil crisis in the 1970's did throw us for a loop, but eventually we fought back, turning our automobile fleet of dirty gas hogs into lean, green machines. Around this time the positive economic impact of globalization kicked into high-gear (more jobs worldwide and lower consumer prices), with strong demand from consumers in two-worker households keeping the economy on the move.

The tech bubble burst in the late 1990's and set us back some, but the combination of deficit spending and the housing bubble kept the economy in motion. When the housing bubble burst in 2007-08, the economy was severely damaged, and the impact of the great recession is still being felt around the world. But we seem to have recovered from even this latest economic disaster, and the global economy, with all its warts, appears as resilient as ever.

THROUGH ALL THE PERIODS of boom and bust over the last eighty years, the wisdom of a 40-hour workweek was seldom questioned, even with both husband and wife now in the workforce. I believe the reasons for this are rooted in our culture, and I'll try to cover that ground in the first few chapters of the book. **Chapters 1** and **2** deal with the importance of work in our lives, as a measure of personal achievement, and as a measure of our contribution to the cooperative community. **Chapter 3** deals with our culture of materialism, with our insatiable desire to acquire more wealth and consume more goods and services, and our apparent disregard for any leisure time to call our own. **Chapter 4** addresses the potential value of that lost leisure time, to individual workers, to families, and to society.

In the next part of the book, I shift gears and talk about the new economy and the implications for work. **Chapter 5** is a discussion about systemic unemployment, industry by industry, as technological advances eliminate whole classes of jobs. **Chapter 6** looks at the impact of globalization on the labor market in the U.S. and around the world. **Chapter 7** is devoted to care providers, and the role of service industries on the new economy.

I next dig into the relationship between employer and employee, or as Adam Smith called them, *master* and *servant*.

Chapter 8 focuses on the adversarial employer vs. employee relationship. In **Chapter 9**, I focus on a problem inherent in the *financialization* of the economy, and how this results in an unhealthy imbalance of power between employer and employee.

Chapter 10 spells out the need to mandate the 24-hour workweek, and offers various approaches to allow the working-poor to work their way out of poverty. The approaches all include a disruptive change to the status quo:

> **Decrease the number of hours worked per week by 40% while increasing the hourly wage by 67%.**

> (This yields the same weekly paycheck for the new "fulltime" worker, but after putting in just 24 hours per week instead of 40.)

Chapter 11 focuses on the need for both employers and employees to manage the change to a shorter workweek. **Chapter 12** closes with the positive impact on society that goes well beyond a partial remedy for systemic unemployment and for dysfunction in the labor market.

I CAN HEAR the loud screams of protest from here – from business owners, from production managers, and from HR directors everywhere – and I openly admit this recalibration is not meant for your benefit. The owner/manager class <u>will</u> take a short-term operational hit as every employer is forced to adjust to the new reality. It will be the hourly employees who are the primary beneficiaries of this proposal in the short-term.

But longer-term, I believe we shall <u>all</u> benefit, as the pervasive impact of trickle-up economics and greater leisure time for all of us takes effect, and as we all again learn how to work to live, not live to work.

CHAPTER 1

Why We Work –
A Brief Historic Overview

WHAT IS WORK? A mechanical engineer will tell us that work, in the most fundamental sense, is applying sufficient force to an object to cause its displacement. $W = F * d$. By that definition, Mother Earth has been hard at work forever – slamming continental plates into each other and blasting molten rock through holes in the crust. Wouldn't it be great if we could go all the way back to Day 1 as a spectator, grab a catbird seat high above our planet, and compress time so that we could observe the entire 4.5-billion-year history of the Earth's tectonic activity in just a few minutes? We would see a very active planet with non-stop earthquake and volcanic activity – continents crashing into each other one minute and ripping apart the next. Mother Earth hard at work, rearranging the deck chairs for her inhabitants, so-to-speak.

But, reverting to real time, the scene becomes much more placid, especially if we peel away the hyperactive layer of atmosphere. The tectonic plates, almost jelly-like in condensed time, now look rock solid. There are occasional volcanic eruptions and rumbling earthquakes, but most of the time and in most places, the surface of the Earth is quite calm. There's a lesson here for all living organisms: If you want to live to be 4.5 billion years old, get lots of rest.

Plants and animals at work

Most living organisms on our fair planet don't have that luxury, of course. In the relatively compressed layer of the biosphere, there is nonstop competition for air, water, and nutrients. Any species that does not work efficiently and diligently will be swept aside, and others will come along and take its place.

Plants work hard to grow and to stay alive, pushing roots deep into the ground to gather water and to access nutrient-rich soils. They cling tenaciously to rocky slopes, penetrate blacktop, find tiny crevices in cement. Trees and vines work to send branches soaring into the morning sky to gather needed sunlight. Flowering plants work feverishly to produce visually attractive blooms – scented displays of eggs and sperm – all designed to enhance the chance of pollination. Plants adapt to their environment and do whatever is necessary to gain a foothold.

Animals, just like plants, work hard to survive. Our animated kin work to find water and food, work to protect themselves from the elements and from predators, and work to reproduce. Reproduction for many animals involves the work of giving birth to live babies (we even call it "going into labor") and actively raising their offspring: nursing the young, bringing them food, protecting them from predators, teaching them to forage and hunt.

All animals that live together in groups, all social animals, take the concept of work a significant step further by engaging in activities that benefit the whole group, not just their immediate families. Edward O. Wilson's book titled *The Social Conquest of Earth*[1] is a marvelous, if controversial, study of the strength of groups in evolution. His focus is on highly social species of animals, those he refers to as *eusocial*, with group members from multiple generations prone to perform altruistic acts as a part of their division of labor.

Many 'higher' order animals that live in herds and packs (including humans) are highly social, but we are late-comers to the scene. Insects predate mammals by 400 million years or so, and some (ants, termites, bees, and wasps) carry out their eusocial duties to a degree that makes us look like bumbling amateurs. Wilson has studied ant colonies extensively, and found that the division of labor is absolute. Whether an ant is gathering food or defending the nest, she will do so "all out", with complete disregard for her personal comfort or safety. All her actions are aimed at the survival of the colony.

Regarding insects' defense of their nests, Wilson states

> *the more elaborate and expensive the nest is in energy and time, the greater the fierceness of the ants to defend it.[2]*

(Something humans can certainly relate to, in spite of the way sunk costs are handled in accounting.)

Homo sapiens – social and biological evolution

Wilson compares the evolution of social insects to that of social humans, and he goes to great lengths to reassure us that we are more than just worker ants. *Homo sapiens* have benefitted from social evolution in concert with biological evolution. We have evolved as both selfish individuals and as altruistic members of groups.

Referring to humans and natural selection, Wilson states that an iron-clad rule exists in genetic social evolution:

It is that selfish individuals beat altruistic individuals, while groups of altruists beat groups of selfish individuals. The victory can never be complete; the balance of selection pressures cannot move to either extreme. If individual selection were to dominate, societies would dissolve. If group selection were to dominate, human groups would come to resemble ant colonies.[3] He goes on *We can expect a continuing conflict between components of behavior favored by individual selection and those favored by group selection.*[4]

Wilson attributes multi-level natural selection (based on behavior that is part-selfish and part altruistic) for the rapid ascent of *Homo sapiens* to our current lofty state, with godlike powers to change our environment and to rule over all other species. Multi-level natural selection means that at a higher level, traits favoring cooperative group behavior are chosen. At the lower level, traits favoring self-serving behavior are chosen. The opposition between the two levels of natural selection has resulted in a *chimeric genotype* in each person. It renders each of us part saint and part sinner.[5]

> *Biological and social evolution have rendered each of us part saint and part sinner.*
>
> *--E.O. Wilson*

Given this dichotomy, part saint and part sinner, what role does work play in our lives? Apparently, there are plenty of reasons why we work, both selfish and altruistic.

ANTHROPOLOGISTS tell us that the genus Homo has been around for over 2 million years.[6] For the great majority of that time (over 99% of our existence) we lived in what we refer to as the Stone Age, a prolonged period marked by the use of the stone tools to enhance hunting and gathering expeditions. (We can safely assume that wooden, leather, and plant-fiber tools were used side-by-side those made of stone, but artifacts made from stone are the only ones to survive the thousands of centuries. Hence the moniker Stone Age.)

As Wilson points out, there was both biological and social evolution during the 2 million years of the Stone Age. The social structure of groups would have evolved. Our ancestors came to live in highly structured clans with divisions of labor designed to benefit the overall wellbeing of the entire clan. We can guess that there would have been chiefs (probably the alpha males) that served as leaders for the clans. There would have been matriarchs managing the camps and the child-rearing activities. There would have been fearless warriors to lead raids of other camps. And there would have been skilled hunters and gatherers to lead foraging expeditions.

All the work performed by members of the clan, those on hunting/gathering expeditions, and those back at camp, contributed to the security and wellbeing of the group. It would have been important for all workers to carry their weight (part saint). Most likely, any slackers would not have been tolerated for long (part sinner). They would've been quickly identified, perhaps given a chance to mend their ways, and if ultimately unable to contribute to the welfare of the clan, ostracized from the group. Thus, social evolution occurred.

Prehistoric man

We have no written record to guide us, but we can make some pretty good guesses on human attitudes about "work" in prehistoric times. We were always highly social animals, of course. Early members of our species, like our primate cousins, went out as teams on cooperative hunting and gathering trips. Successful expeditions resulted in bounty to be shared with the rest of the clan. Other clan members not participating on hunting or foraging expeditions would be engaged in work activities back at camp that benefitted the group – child-bearing, child-rearing, and defense of the "nest". These cooperative activities, aimed at survival of the group, were probably not thought of as work, just as living.

But the life of these early humans was not meant to stay so pure and simple. The clans were hierarchal, and it is easy to imagine scenarios where certain individuals (maybe the tribal chiefs, maybe the priests) ordered those lower in the pecking order to do things for them. The alpha males may order underlings to fetch food and water, to gather material for shelter, probably even to enforce intra-group discipline on their behalf. The underlings would comply because the elite had more important things to do – higher "value-added" governing or spiritual activities.

SOMEWHERE ALONG THE LINE, these early human subordinates, quite capable of sentient thought, probably <u>did</u> start to think of subservient duties as <u>work</u>, activity they'd rather not be engaged in if they had a choice.

While some of the workers probably rendered these services quite willingly (just happy to be associated with the big dog!), others probably grumbled along the way. Either way, I am guessing they thought of these activities in service to higher ranking individuals in a manner quite differently from the everyday hunting, gathering, and childrearing tasks that they associated with life itself. I imagine that at least some of these individuals thought about those subservient activities as <u>work</u>, an activity that had a negative connotation.

AS ALL THIS WAS HAPPENING, other lines of work were being born. Certain individuals would have been recognized as especially good tool makers, tools made of stone, wood, and leather. They fashioned hammers from rocks that made it easier to crack open bones and nuts. They chiseled spears and knives that made the hunt more lethal and skinning the animals easier. Those weapons that were made for the hunt were also very useful for offensive raids on other clans and for defense of the home camp.

These technological advancements made the tribe more efficient as hunters and gatherers, and made life on the savannah that much easier. The tribe was better off to have the stone-cutters and leather-workers stay home and make more tools that all could use than to send these artisans out on hunting expeditions. The specialization of labor was born. This division of labor resulted in more weapons for everyone which made the clan a stronger force and more secure within their territory. The tool makers would have thus earned esteem for their skills and effort, and respect for their handiwork. Was this the birth of the mercantile class?

Tool making would have become a designated "occupation" for those skilled in the craft, and that work would have been thought of much differently from those jobs in direct service to the tribal elite.

My guess is that very early on, humans took the concept of work (activities performed to benefit the clan that fall outside those normally associated with life itself) and began to assign value to it. Greater value for some work (hammering out spear points), lesser value for other (fetching wood for the fire). While all this work was important for the survival of the clan, there was probably a greater appreciation for the contribution of the stone cutters than for that of the firewood gatherers.

The tool-makers would've gravitated to that specialty because they were good at the job and they enjoyed their creative work. During times of abundance, instead of going out on hunting expeditions, they probably had the freedom to stay home and keep puttering around the rock quarry to see what new and different items they could come up with. The iPhone maybe.

THIS "PRIMITIVE" LIFESTYLE went on for about 2 million years, remember. It was only with the onset of agriculture about 12,000 years ago that life for humans began to resemble what we now think of as normal.

At some point back in that timeframe, agricultural practices became more important than hunting/gathering, and with that development permanent settlements began to appear. This would've resulted in an explosion of occupational specialties, each carrying more or less social and self-esteem than the next. All of this is conjecture, of course. It would be another 10,000 years before we started writing things down.

HERBERT APPLEBAUM produced a comprehensive study of the role of work in our lives in a book titled *The Concept of Work*.[7] The book chronologically tracks the meaning of work from the ancient world, through the middle ages, to modern times. Applebaum relies on the written record for his commentary, though he admits

> *People who work are mostly humble, with no voice in the recorded pages from which histories are written. It is mostly the leisured or the recipients of the state's or a patron's largesse who have the time, energy, and training to produce written works.*[8]

With that disclaimer, it is nonetheless instructive to look back at how work was perceived throughout history.

The ancient world

Applebaum begins his study of the concept of work with Homeric Greece. Two occupations were held in greatest esteem – farming and soldiering. Craftsmen were next in the hierarchy. At the bottom were traders and merchants – those engaged in commercial activities between households. The notion was that the agrarian households were supposed to be self-sufficient, therefore commercial trading between the farms was probably seen as a necessary evil, and somehow ancillary to the core activities that guaranteed the survival of the household.

Slavery was deeply embedded in those ancient economies, but that was a status of non-citizenship, not an occupation. A slave may have been a teacher, a craftsman, a servant, a soldier, or all of the above; and his relative status would have reflected the work he performed on behalf of his master. Indeed, many slaves were probably more secure in life than many free working men. After all, the master had quite an investment in slaves that he owned as he kept them fed, clothed, and sheltered so they could continue to perform their duties. But the freeman merchant in the market was on his own, and if he fell on hard times, he had no one else to depend on for his livelihood.

FARMERS AND SOLDIERS were also held in high esteem in the Roman Empire. To understand why this would've been true, look at parallels in Wilson's eusocial ant colonies: with human farmers analogous to foraging ants, and with soldiers of both species defending the nest. For the human soldiers, the "nest" being defended grew from the Greek city-state to the Roman Empire. Whether farming or soldiering, these most basic survival activities were not thought of as servile work, but as essential survival skills, critical for the life of the community. They were, therefore, placed on a higher plain than mercantile trade activities.

But highly esteemed or not, all work that contributed to the welfare of the community would've been considered important, and all community members would've been expected to participate. Even the nobles performed work on their family estate, perhaps to set a good example for the working class slaves and freemen if nothing else.

The middle ages

As we moved into medieval times, Applebaum shows that the attitude toward work in the middle ages is dominated by Jewish and Christian philosophy. In the very first book of the bible we are taught that God himself worked for six straight days to create our world before resting on day seven. Down here on Earth, Applebaum tells us that the Jews *respected the free workers, and treated the slave with consideration. They taught that a man is entitled to his wages on the same day he worked and that it is a sin to defraud a man of his wage.*[9]

This general attitude toward work is carried forward by the early Christians, and they viewed all work as important, including manual labor. They stressed the responsibility for all community members to contribute to the general welfare of the community. Indeed, in St. Paul's second letter to the Thessalonians, we find this edict:

Now we command you brethren, in the name of our Lord Jesus Christ, that you keep away from any brother who is living in idleness... (II Thessalonians 3:6).

St. Augustine carried this attitude quite a step further, introducing the concept of working explicitly for charitable purposes (*it is more blessed to give than to receive*). For Augustine, economic gain is never an end in itself.

Any fruits of work over and above those which suffice for a frugal life, should not be allowed to accumulate, but should be given to the indigent.[10]

Throughout the middle ages, religious monasteries became the most socially significant institutions in many localities. Monastic life was highly structured, governed by strict schedules of prayer and work:

The Rule of St. Benedict *legislated minutely for the employment of every hour of the day according to the season of the year. It prescribed the time for work, prayer, reading, dinner, a siesta, and meditation. The weak and the strong must work, although consideration is given to the weak in the selection of the appropriate work for them.*[11]

The raison d'être of the monasteries was to serve God, and when the monks did their chores diligently, they became servants of God. The disciplined approach to life made the monasteries models of domestic efficiency. And if the highly structured day was good for many of the monks, it was certainly good for the abbot, making management of the monastery a much easier task.

These lessons were not lost in the secular world. Steady hard work equaled economic progress.

The modern world

The renaissance in Europe moved us into the modern world – artistically, scientifically, and philosophically. Our attitude toward work moved forward as well, significantly shaped by the Protestant Reformation and the teachings of Martin Luther and John Calvin. According to the writings of Applebaum:

> *Luther's originality was in his idea that one best serves God by doing most perfectly the work of one's trade or profession. With this idea, Luther swept away the concept that there was a distinction between spiritual work and secular work—a belief which was prevalent in the middle ages.*
>
> *All work contributes to the common life of mankind. Hence, no one is more necessary than another to piety and blessedness.*[12]

Appelbaum tells us that Calvin added substantially to Luther's proclamation, giving us the backbone of the protestant work ethic:

> *With Calvin comes a new attitude toward labor. All men,
> including the rich, must work because to work is the will
> of God. But they must not lust after the fruits of their
> work. With this new creed comes a new type of man—
> strong-willed, active, austere, and hard-working from
> religious conviction. Idleness, luxury, prodigality—
> everything that softens the soul—is shunned. Dislike of
> work is a sign that one is not destined for salvation.*

> *Puritanism—which developed from Calvinism—goes
> further, teaching that it is one's duty to extract the greatest
> possible gain from work. Success, which is proven by
> profit, is the certain indication that the chosen profession
> is pleasing to God.*[13]

Richard Donkin, in his book *Blood, Sweat & Tears,* tells us
that two hundred years after Calvin, Thomas Carlyle wrote
about the *goodness* of work in and of itself:

> *All true work is sacred; in all true work, were it but true
> hard labor, there is something of the divineness.*

Donkin writes that a century later, John Stuart Mill
thought this was nonsense. He wrote:

> *Work, I imagine, is not a good in itself. There is nothing
> laudable about work for work's sake.*[14]

It should be apparent by now that I place myself squarely in the
Mill camp.

The modern world brought new political realities into being
as well. John Locke argued for *universal birthrights* which
granted each citizen the right to defend his *life, health, liberty,
and property* from the divine-rights claims of royalty. Thomas
Jefferson leaned on Locke's convictions when he added his trio

of *universal rights* to the Declaration of Independence: *life, liberty, and the pursuit of happiness.*

These developments laid the groundwork for the industrial revolution.

The industrial revolution

About 200 years after Martin Luther published his 95 theses in a letter to his superior (apparently, he did not defiantly nail them to the church door in Wittenberg, but perhaps posted them on a bulletin board for discussion)[15], the first machines of the industrial revolution sprang into life. Thereafter, life for factory workers would never be the same. Prior to the industrial revolution, the need for workers was defined by natural rhythms, day-to-day, and throughout the year. With industrialization came large, mechanically powered and artificially lit factories. These were capital intensive facilities, and as such it was economically prudent to keep them running as much as possible.

If the protestant reformation gave us the spiritual reasons to work (to serve God), it was the industrial revolution that *allowed* us to work around the clock. The foundation for modern capitalism is thus laid.

Working conditions for many in the early years of the industrial revolution were brutishly nasty, yet men, women, and children subjected themselves to these awful conditions because 1) they had little choice in the matter, and 2) employment offered a chance (a remote chance) to escape their wretched status in life.

Man, as machine

In the late nineteenth and early twentieth centuries, Frederick Winslow Taylor and other proponents of *scientific management* did their very best to reduce the tasks of factory workers to the clockwork of machinery. Taylor looked back at progress made in the previous century of the industrial revolution and recognized that machines were responsible for the tremendous growth in productivity, and the steady rise in prosperity for the common man. Furthermore, he concluded that the closer we could get factory workers to behave as reliably as machines, the better off everyone would be. He was convinced that this would not happen automatically. Just the opposite, Taylor expected factory workers to slack off, if given the chance.

Taylor's approach was to reduce every manual labor task to discreet steps that could be standardized, measured, and timed. With the scientific management of labor, the output of factory workers could be as predictable as that of the machines they tended.

Taylor was indubitably right – the factory owners and consumers would be far better off. The factory workers, on the other hand, were reduced to well-oiled pieces of machinery, and the employees in those factories now had just as much autonomy as the machines.

Why did production employees put up with this kind of abuse? I'll spend a good part of the book trying to answer that question. For now, suffice it to say that at least part of the answer lies in the fact that the producers of factory goods are also the consumers of those goods.

This mentality – factory workers as cogs in a machine – held firm throughout the first half of the twentieth century. It wasn't until post WWII that this cold and calculated treatment of employees began to be seriously examined.

Man, as master of machine

During WWII, the dire need for wartime production completely outweighed any concern for the niceties in the work environment. But once the war was over and the soldiers and sailors returned to the workforce, concern for the social welfare of shop-floor workers began to take root.

Many were unhappy with the single-minded mechanistic processes of Taylorism, including, quite notably, Abraham Maslow. Maslow's assumptions about workers were diametrically opposed to Taylor's:

> *Assume that everyone is to be trusted.*
>
> *Assume the preference for working rather than being idle.*
>
> *All human beings prefer meaningful work to meaningless work.*[16]

This trust in the worker and the focus on his welfare was long overdue. We'll spend more time on that topic in the next chapter.

Conclusion

Why do we work? Just like all the other plants and animals we share this planet with, we work to live, to survive and to thrive. For over 99% of our existence, that meant hunting and gathering for our food, clothing and shelter needs. In times of abundance, that work was easy, and we probably did not think of these activities as work at all – just as living. In challenging times, when the environment turned inhospitable, working just to survive would have been very hard indeed.

In both good times and bad we were engaged in other kinds of work beyond hunting and gathering expeditions, other activities that benefitted the whole clan, not just ourselves and our families: these included shared cooking, shelter-building, and child-rearing activities. The work of our esteemed tool makers was offered as example.

There was another kind of more subservient work – personal service offered by lower-ranking clan members to the clan superiors. We can assume that at some point, well before recorded history, that type of work took on religious overtones, as in: *your service to the priest is also service to god himself*. And the priest, of course, would constantly remind everyone that keeping the gods happy would benefit the whole community. Throughout ancient times, the concept of work would have included all those activities we perform that benefit the whole community, not just ourselves.

As we moved into the agricultural period and the increasing complexity of permanent settlements, the types of work performed on behalf of the whole community would've evolved substantially. To keep track of the relative value of everyone's contributions, we moved beyond barter systems, beyond the use of cattle and grain as mediums of exchange. We invented money. We now had a handy mechanism to keep track of commercial trade, and a useful method of retaining excess profits. This allowed us to create personal wealth that went beyond one's status at birth.

With technological development (going all the way back to the Bronze Age 5000 years ago), the demand for manufactured products created a need for production workers. This really blossomed with the industrial revolution (300 years ago) and work became an avenue for lower class families to accumulate wealth and move into a more comfortable middle class lifestyle. For a fortunate few, work was an avenue to upper class comfort.

THROUGHOUT RECORDED HISTORY, work has been a means of *serving. Self-serving,* of course, but also serving the *community,* and in many cases, serving *god and country.* Work is an important way to establish our self-worth and our contributions as a member of the community. Our occupation has become a crucial part of our very identity.

CHAPTER 2

Working Today –
Our Occupation – Our Identity

IT IS SUCH A JOY to see and hear children on a playground. They are so full of life, uninhibited, and unencumbered by the stress of our adult world. Yet role-playing as an adult is a favorite activity among children everywhere. And the specific occupations they chose tell us a lot about ourselves. Teachers, naturally, are a favorite because most kids like their teachers, and the teacher gets to be boss! Other roles you might hear the kids playing are policeman and fireman, positions with authority and respect, plus they have those cool uniforms.

Children will choose many adult roles to play because they sound fun, and because the jobs carry an air of respect. Jobs like astronaut and archeologist—that would be so cool! Kids understand, intuitively, that an occupation is an important part of establishing one's identity and status within the community. They look up to teachers and firemen and astronauts; and they want the other kids to look up to them.

What will you not hear out on the playground? You will not hear the kids assuming the role of a down-trodden welder who lost his job when the shipyard closed last year. Nor a laid-off factory worker, nor a down-sized office worker, nor an overworked (and undervalued) retail clerk. <u>Not</u> fun and <u>not</u> cool.

The mysterious process of selecting an occupation

What kind of careers young children dream about will depend a lot on the accident of their birth. A boy from the Dominican Republic may grow up with dreams of becoming a major league baseball player, but probably not an NHL hockey star. That's a trivial example, but we can think of another, just as telling, and more insidiously limiting: A young girl from a public housing high-rise may imagine herself growing up to be a hair stylist, but without any first-hand knowledge of adults who are executives in the business world, it's unlikely that she'll dream about growing up to become a bank president. And that's too bad because she would probably make an excellent bank president if given half the chance. (Not that she wouldn't be a great hair stylist too.) But the types of jobs kids will initially role-play will be limited to those within the scope of their family's personal experience, and what they are exposed to on the school playground.

As children grow older, they meet more kids and other families, and this broadens the scope of careers they can aim for. Likewise, through our culture (television, movies, books), children are exposed to an ever-growing selection of job possibilities. The possibilities of what a child can grow up to "be" should expand greatly as they get older.

Almost all this process, I believe, happens informally. There are guidance counselors in schools. But my sense is that their impact on a student's career selection is quite uneven. I believe the influence of family and classmates plays a bigger role.

When it comes to occupational options, there should be no limitations on what is possible. But we see, quickly, a sorting out of students by academic achievement level. Some will zoom ahead with reading, writing, and math. Others will struggle. Those who struggle will respond in one of two ways. They'll push themselves even harder, attempting to keep up with their peers. Or they'll realize, with dejection, that some career paths may not be an option for them.

This sorting-out occurs all through the school years, and is accelerated as a child moves from elementary school to middle school to high school. Once a young adult reaches college, the occupational choices still under consideration will really make a difference in what classes he takes. And in college, most students prepare themselves quite well for jobs in the 'adult' world, or to enter grad school in a specific field.

But there are still many, as I can personally attest, who traipse blissfully through four years of liberal arts education without a clue what they want to do when they 'grow up'.

That's OK. There are now literally hundreds of potential careers to choose from. Over 800 in fact. And if a person is curious enough, the U.S. Department of Labor tracks unique occupations – everything from Accountants to Zoologists.[17] DOL keeps a treasure trove of statistics on each occupation. How many are employed, where they are employed, who employs them, and average annual salaries. The DOL data is amazingly detailed and freely accessed. Just reading through the list should get one's imaginative juices flowing. Actuary? There's a career you can count on. Audiologist? I hear that's a good job. (don't groan!)

The two largest categories in the DOL database are Retail Sales Person (4.6M) and Cashier (3.4M). Unfortunately, these occupations are on the low end of the scale for average annual salaries: $25,760 and $20,640 respectively. Furthermore, the retail world is rife with bad jobs. Not only is the pay low relative to most other parts of our economy. The schedules of work are among the poorest and the least reliable. Lots of retail establishments are open 24/7, and you can plan on working evenings and weekends when everyone else is off the clock.

Actually, you may be on the schedule for the coming weekend, but you could get a call from your boss at the last minute telling you that he doesn't need you after all. So don't plan on spending that paycheck quite yet.

BUT WITH OVER 800 unique occupations to choose from, why settle for Cashier, Retail Sales Person, or Firefighter? As new occupations are added, others are dropped, some very quickly. For instance, you won't find any Keypunchers on employment rolls today, while as recently as 1980 you could still find that position featured on workflow charts.

The DOL forecast for the two fastest growing occupations between 2010 and 2020 are Personal Care Aides *(70% growth)* and Home Health Aides *(69%)*, important services, and unlikely to be eliminated by automation. But unfortunately, just like many retail positions, these are two careers toward the very bottom of the pay scale *(around $20K/yr)*. More about the impact of this later.

Types of work arrangements and connections between employer and employee

Moving on from how occupations are selected, I want to spend a moment now to discuss the various modes of employment, the ways one can be a participant in the workforce: as a slave, an indentured servant, an intern, an employee, an independent contractor, or as self-employed. (Volunteers are not included, even though they create a ton of economic value for their organizations, because they are not reimbursed for their efforts, and for the purposes of this book, are not at "work" while volunteering.)

At the very bottom of the employment pyramid we find slavery – an institution still accepted in certain backwater parts of the world. Slaves are literally owned by their employees. As such, they can be sold or traded like any other economic resource. Slaves have no say in the tasks they are asked to perform on the job. They cannot choose where they work, who they work for, or what they do. It is easy to see why those trapped in slavery will risk life and limb to escape.

Other than slaves, and their economic cousins indentured servants, most of us in the workforce are there by choice. We are employees, and we come in dozens of flavors: hourly and salaried; tipped and non-tipped; permanent, seasonal, and temporary; fulltime and part time; with full benefits and no benefits; those with and without profit sharing or employee stock purchase plans. Employers design compensation packages to attract and retain good employees and to reward them for their service to the company. It is pretty much a cold economic transaction – my labor in exchange for your compensation. It wasn't always so.

Benjamin Disraeli wrote a fine novel about England during the industrial revolution. In his book *Sybil, or The Two Nations*, we read about Mr. Trafford, an enlightened factory owner

> *With gentle blood in his veins, and old English feelings, he imbibed, at an early period of his career, a correct conception of the relations which should subsist between the employer and the employed. He felt that between them*

there should be other ties than the payment and the receipt of wages.

Trafford established housing for the workers where they could live for a reasonable fee, and his own home was right in the middle of the village:

> *And what was the influence of such an employer and such a system of employment on the morals and manners of the employed? Great: infinitely beneficial. The connexion of a labourer with his place of work, whether agricultural or manufacturing, is itself a vast advantage. Proximity to the employer brings cleanliness and order, because it brings observation and encouragement.* [18]

But lest we think the situation in England in 1837 idyllic, Disraeli makes this observation on the open design of Trafford's factory:

> *the child works under the eye of the parent, the parent under that of the superior workman; the inspector or employer at a glance can behold all.*

(It is the *child works* part caught my eye. In the modern world, we do not allow children in the workforce anymore. No moral ambiguity about that in my mind. But we should acknowledge, this is a relatively recent development.)

Disraeli's intimate, paternal relationship between employer and employee is a far cry from that between employer and employee today. Indeed, companies are apt to hire workers on "alternative work arrangements" nowadays rather than as employees with a full suite of benefits. In a column by Robert Samuelson, we learn that these include workers in four categories:

1. *Independent contractors and freelancers, usually self-employed, from writers to software engineers*
2. *On-call workers who have designated days when they may (or may not) be summoned on the job—a practice common in fast food*
3. *Workers from temporary work agencies*
4. *Workers provided by contract firms—cafeteria and security services being examples.*[19]

These "alternative" workers are a rapidly growing segment of the workforce, from 10.7% of all jobs in 2005 to 15.8% in 2015. Roughly one out of six new hires. Other than the first category of independent contractors, it seems unlikely that many of the other workers are intentionally choosing those routes. More likely, these are workers that large and small companies can hire and fire on a whim, and to whom they don't have to pay benefits.

Again, this is a cold, hard economic calculation. Nothing paternalistic about these arrangements.

Self-employed is a unique employment status. Both the boss and underling, employer and employee, one truly in charge of their own destiny (or so they hope). Many of the self-employed who become successful drive themselves relentlessly, and like authors and artists, they can be their own worst critics.

But this book is not about or for the self-employed. This book is about employees, and interns, and those four categories of alternative workers listed above. The book focuses on the number of hours of labor these workers put in, and the compensation they receive for their efforts.

Specialization

Going back to DOL's list of over 800 careers to choose from, theoretically, as an individual's job description becomes more and more specialized, the organization that employs that worker makes more efficient use of their unique talents and capabilities. By extension, the larger community and the entire economy benefit as well.

But a high degree of specialization can also result in certain pitfalls. An individual's job may become so narrow, so focused on minutia, that it becomes hard to keep the big picture in mind. He may find himself wondering: *Why does all this even matter?*

Employees who have a broader range of job responsibilities, those who *wear many hats* at work, are in a naturally better position to keep the overall mission of the organization in mind, and of finding their job to be meaningful. This is easy to see in a high-tech start-up where a handful of brilliant engineers may put in 60 – 80-hour weeks creating a new product. Early on, all are gung-ho. But as the start-up morphs into a successful, mature company, the engineers' individual jobs probably become much more defined, more constrained; and unfortunately for some, less personally meaningful. Yet, that 60 – 80-hour workweek mentality persists.

Small jobs

Being a tiny cog in a giant machine is one form of specialization, I guess, but not one most workers will want to strive for. Before the advent of the industrial revolution, things were made by hand by craftsmen. The shoemaker started with a piece of tanned leather. He cut and stretched and shaped and sewed, until he ended up with a pair of shoes. That had to be a quite satisfying as a vocation.

With the industrial revolution, we started to make things with machines, in large factories, with lots of workers. Human labor became an extension of machine power. Men, women, and children were employed to load and unload machines. Keeping up with the pace of the machine was their only task. A lot of us would find these factory jobs mind-numbingly boring:

1. *Grab part from bin and place in the machine.*
2. *Push button.*
3. *Pull finished part from machine and place in another bin.*
4. *Repeat.*

Karl Marx referred to this as the *immiseration* of factory workers stuck on the same task day in and day out.

Frederick Taylor reduced the study of these simple tasks to a science, with the output of the worker scrutinized the same way as the powered equipment. With this kind of knowledge, manufacturers were able to design assembly lines – complex "machines" that employed whole line-ups of workers on narrow, repetitive jobs.

The immiseration of factory workers has been covered by several authors. Donkin tells us about one of the characters in Studs Terkel's great book *Working* who put the workers' condition like this:

> *Most of us, like the assembly line worker, have jobs that are too small for our spirit. Jobs are not big enough for people."*[20]

Jobs that are too small seem all too commonplace in the economy today

Chris Farrell in his book *Unretirement* finds another way this can be expressed with this wonderful quote from H. L. Mencken:

If he got no reward whatsoever, the artist would go on working just the same; his actual reward, in fact, is often so little that he almost starves. But suppose a garment worker got nothing for his labor: would he go on working just the same? Can one imagine his submitting voluntarily to hardship and sore that he might express his soul in 200 more pairs of ladies pants? [21]

Farrell is not dismissing the importance of work – just small jobs. In a column for the NY Times[22], he writes that working longer can result in better health outcomes. He's not talking about working longer hours each day, but longer into life, into what had previously been thought of as retirement years. Keeping the body and brain active is good for us, of course. More important are the benefits of continued social interactions – with your boss, co-workers, suppliers, and customers. Smaller jobs (those without cognitive challenge and with fewer positive human interactions), will have much less of a benefit to our mental health.

Eliminating *cog-in-the-machinery* jobs wherever possible will be good for the human spirit. One hundred years after Frederick Taylor's "scientific management" and Henry Ford's assembly line, the factory worker is no longer just a well-oiled piece of machinery. He is now CNC literate, studies 6-sigma quality methods, and squeezes every last pound of productivity out of every ounce of input. The factory worker, much like the shoemaker before the industrial revolution, once again has a meaningful job. That's the good news. The bad news is that while it used to take hundreds of workers to keep a factory running, it now takes just a handful.

A lot of those factory jobs have shifted to the retail sector. That's the focus in Zeynep Ton's book *The Good Jobs Strategy*[23]. She divides the retail world, rather definitively, into two parts: companies who pursue a *good jobs strategy,* and companies who follow a *bad jobs strategy*. Companies in the first group understand that their employees are valuable partners who need and deserve good jobs. Those in the second think of employees as necessary cost centers, and the less attention spent on them, the better.

One of the most egregious sins of companies in the *bad jobs* camp is their cavalier attitude about employees' work schedules. Amy Lindgren, with the St. Paul Pioneer Press, covered this ground beautifully in a heartfelt column on the importance of reliable work schedules.[24] Lindgren asks: without knowing when we are supposed to be working, how can anyone live their lives? Specifically, how can anyone schedule activities that have a chance of improving their economic status? Activities that are especially important to low-income workers – like going to school, looking for a better job, or holding down a second job? A schedule that bounces around from week-to-week, or worse yet, a requirement to be available on-call just in case you are needed to work, make it extremely difficult for the working poor. Lindgren wraps up the column by saying:

No one can climb a career ladder
when someone keeps moving the
base around.
--Amy Lindgren

Career advancement

If we work in a large company, the position we hold within the organizational hierarchy carries a lot of weight: supervisor—manager—director—president—CEO. Each of these titles represents a succession of greater responsibility and authority, successively larger paychecks, and higher levels of prestige. When it comes to climbing corporate ladders, how high is high enough? It's a very personal thing, but for some ambitious individuals there is no such thing as "high enough". Ayn Rand put it this way:

Man's ego is the fountainhead of human progress.
--Ayn Rand

Climbing up the employment ladder is important for all of us as we enter the workforce – for financial reasons, and for the honor and prestige associated with our job title. In extreme cases, career advancement itself becomes the raison d'être for the ambitious worker. (*Think about that a minute. That worker is not interested in the mission of the organization except insofar as it benefits him personally. He's driven by his personal career advancement.*) We may personally feel that we are above that sort of single-minded ambition, but it does explain how climbing the corporate ladder has become competitive sport.

An entry-level employee may be pretty satisfied with their brand new job. But if they find themselves in exactly the same position some years down the road, their level of satisfaction will drop off substantially. On the other hand, if they make some progress advancing within the organization, and at least keep up with their peers, they will most likely be satisfied with their careers.

Like many things in life, your perception of success climbing the career ladder is all relative, and will depend on your personal expectations and those of your immediate circle of friends and family. If you hope to someday make the rank of foreman and one day you achieve that goal, you will call that a successful career. But if you are convinced that nothing short of plant superintendent is acceptable, achieving the rank of foreman after a long, dedicated career just won't cut it.

IT USED TO BE that young adults would start out at "the plant" or "the firm" shortly after completing high school or college. It was expected that they would work hard, play by the rules, and climb the corporate ladder rung-by-rung, all the way up to the point where the Peter Principle kicked in. If a person didn't play by the rules and tried to skip a rung or two, he'd probably be labeled "*not a team play*er" and get knocked down a peg or two. If a person didn't exhibit the proper amount of drive, he'd be marked "*lacks ambition*", an even more damning status.

Nowadays, careers are not nearly so linear. First, we seldom see anyone staying with a single company throughout their working lives. Second, career moves can be up, down, sideways. This is now commonplace, and there is no longer the same stigma associated with a "step down". (This may relieve some of the trepidation experienced leading up to 10 and 20-year class reunions.) (Interestingly, by the 40th reunion, little of that seems to matter anymore. Being able to brag about our grandkids is much more important.)

NOT JUST OUR EGO is at stake when it comes to career advancement. The size of our paycheck is directly impacted by how far we advance within our field of work. In an ideal world, our paycheck at work would be a direct reflection of our value to the company. As everyone knows, we do not live in an ideal world, and in later chapters I address what I believe are inequalities in the way workers are compensated.

Meaningful jobs

Meaningful jobs and *good bosses* go hand-in-hand. The easiest way to see this is in the position of domestic servant. In these one-on-one employment arrangements, you might, if you are lucky, find yourself with a boss you'd be willing to give your life for. Or you may have a boss you feel like strangling several times each day. In a love-hate employment relationship, this may be the same guy. Your job as his servant certainly has meaning in either event.

Most of us are not employed in one-on-one situations like this. We work for companies that employ tens, hundreds, even thousands of workers; all engaged to make the products and provide the services that the company offers. If we know what the company does, and why – if we understand the overall mission of the organization we work for and find that to be in sync with our personal beliefs – it will be much easier to feel that our jobs are meaningful. If not, the job is just a source of income, perhaps one we are dispassionate about, perhaps one we hate. And like being stuck in a job with a boss we don't relate to, this is bound to cause some personal discord.

It is the responsibility of everyone in a supervisory position to do more than just show how the work is to be done. It is every supervisor's responsibility to explain why the work is being done, to make sure every worker knows the mission of the company, and how, in a larger sense, the organization contributes to the welfare of the community. Without this knowledge, there is a danger that we find our jobs to be unimportant except for the paycheck, and not worthy of our sincerest efforts.

Given a company that provides goods and services useful to society, we then look for these attributes of a meaningful job (from Hackman and Oldham): *1) the chance to use a variety of skills, 2) the chance to see the job through from beginning to end, and 3) the chance to do something that makes a difference.*[25]

Let's go back to the pre-industrial revolution shoemaker again. He employs a number of skills in his craft and transforms a shapeless piece of leather into a pair of shoes – a very important pair of shoes indeed for whoever the lucky customer is. Compare that with performing a single task on a long assembly line.

I am not a Luddite. I don't believe we should go back to making shoes by hand, except as a craft. That is not the way to make sure all seven billion of us have access to an affordable pair of shoes. But building machines to make our shoes and shirts and trousers doesn't mean we can't find some way for all of us to be engaged in meaningful work.

Cleaning an office building can be meaningful work if you have the right attitude, the right boss, and you work in the right environment. Dan Teran, the chief executive of a cleaning service company called *Managed by Q*[26], may be the right boss. Teran, with a tip of his hat to Zeynep Ton's 'good jobs strategy', pays his cleaners more than the prevailing wage. He knows happy employees make a better workforce. While *Managed by Q* is primarily a building cleaning service, they offer other, higher value-added services too. Teran knows that his cleaners are the ones in contact with his customers, becoming, in effect, everyday sales reps for his firm. The other contracts they win (for cleaning supplies, for pest extermination, for furniture moving and assembly) more than pay for the higher wages he pays the cleaners.

Teran believes

that decades of rising inequality and stagnant wages in America are not an inevitable byproduct of capitalism;

41

instead, they come from a simple misunderstanding about how to best deploy workers and recognize the value they bring to the company.[27]

Good bosses and bad bosses can make all the difference. A good supervisor can make any job feel worthwhile, be it working on an assembly line, at a retail checkout counter, or cleaning offices.

To summarize, we find this very succinct definition of *meaningful work* from Barry Schwartz in a column in the NY Times:

Of course, we care about our wages, and we wouldn't work without them. But we care about more than money. We want work that is challenging and engaging, that enables us to exercise some discretion and control over what we do, and that provides us opportunities to learn and grow. We want to work with colleagues who we respect and with supervisors who respect us. Most of all, we want work that is meaningful – that makes a difference to other people and thus ennobles us in at least some small way.[28]

Unemployment

It is precisely the ennobling aspect of work that makes the status of unemployment so devastating. Wherever we find ourselves in our work careers, relatively high up on the totem pole or down at ground level, just having a job is critical to our well-being.

Buckminster Fuller had other ideas about this. In an interview back in 1970, he said:

We should do away with the absolutely specious notion that everybody has to earn a living. It is a fact today that one in ten thousand of us can make a technological breakthrough capable of supporting all the rest. The youth of today are absolutely right in recognizing this nonsense of earning a living. We keep inventing jobs because of this false idea that everybody has to be employed at some kind of drudgery because, according to Malthusian Darwinian theory, he must justify his right to exist. So we have inspectors of inspectors and people making instruments for inspectors to inspect inspectors. The true business of people should be to go back to school and think about whatever it was they were thinking about before someone came along and told them they had to earn a living.[29]

Bucky Fuller was on the right track, but I think he was missing some of the fundamental reasons why we all feel the need to work. We work for more than Darwinian *red in tooth and claw* reasons of survival. We actually <u>do</u> feel the need to justify our right to exist, and there are social, even eusocial reasons to work. (See E. O. Wilson)

Ironic as it sounds, it is exactly because work is so important in our culture that we should all work a little less. This gives everyone a better chance to avoid unemployment and keep a paid position during down-turns in the economy and during labor markets thick and thin. Economists tell us that bouts of

Unemployment is not an equal-opportunity employer.

--George Borjas

high unemployment hit some classes of workers much harder than others. Younger workers suffer more than older. Less-educated more than those with more education. Blacks and

43

Hispanics more than whites. And some industries harder than others (for example, construction workers are typically hit harder than government workers). Until recently, women were hit with more unemployment than men, although that has reversed itself in the last few decades.

George Borjas, in his textbook *Labor Economics*, classifies unemployment by types:

- **Frictional**. The natural result of the labor market being in a constant state of flux. There's always some delay when a worker leaves one job (whether voluntarily or not) and signs up for another.
- **Seasonal**. Agricultural unemployment an easy example. Retail unemployment following the Christmas shopping season another.
- **Cyclical**. An imbalance in the number of workers and the amount of work available as we enter a recession.
- **Structural**. As automation eliminates whole classes of jobs, and as old industries fade away, there is a surplus of workers and a mismatch between the skills that workers are supplying and the skills employers are looking for.[30] (This type of unemployment is most pernicious, and is covered in some depth in Chapter 5.)

Unemployment benefits from the government do help alleviate the financial burden of the condition, but they do not alleviate the stigma associated with unemployment. We are social animals, and we feel we need to work, to be contributing members of society. To be unemployed is embarrassing because we are taking from society, not giving.

If a worker is downsized from a large corporation, he is not normally dumped immediately out on the street. He'll be placed on the surplus list and given some time (up to 6 months) to find a new position, either within the company or out. But as anyone who has been in that situation can attest, <u>that</u> is just about the worst job in the world! And ironically, this is a case where being on the high end of the corporate ladder may be a disadvantage. The pool of jobs that are available to an unemployed executive shrinks rapidly as one moves from the manager level to director to VP.

When unemployment is widespread, the whole community suffers. Indeed, we've seen communities small and large die for lack of work. Small towns in rural America dried up and blew away during the farm crisis. Entire neighborhoods in big cities did the same as large factories shut down and all the jobs were lost.

Work is critical to our financial and emotional wellbeing. When we encounter systematic unemployment, it is damaging to both individual and communal psyche. Bill and Melinda Gates understand the importance of work, and they place it front-and-center of the activities of their Foundation with the tagline:

Giving all of us the chance to live happy and productive lives.

Work for people with disabilities

I was able to see real world evidence of the importance of work while employed at Merrick, Inc., a nonprofit social services and vocational program in Vadnais Heights, MN. Merrick serves adults with intellectual/developmental disabilities, all of whom were eligible for monthly Social Security disability payments, and none of whom had to work. Yet, work was exactly what they wanted from our company. Our clients watched as family members and friends went to work every day, and they observed their co-workers at Merrick on the job. They understood, intuitively, that it is through paid employment that we become members of the community in good standing.

45

To fail on a job is not the same thing as failing to be a good worker. This is especially true when it comes to finding the right job for an adult with a disability. Merrick provides vocational services for adults with diagnoses ranging from moderate to profound. Although cognitively disabled, many of the individuals we served understood the importance of working and earning a paycheck. Many had a very solid grasp on the fundamental constructs of what we find important in life – spirituality, friendship, community, and service; and they intuitively understood that by working and earning a paycheck, they were participating fully and being contributing members of society.

Working in this field, I learned that there are not disabled adults, there are adults with disabilities. It is a subtle, but important difference. We are all human beings, first and foremost. And I learned that no one is fully disabled. Conversely, no one is fully able-bodied and able-minded. This is not a binary system, and all of us have disabilities in one manner or another.

If you are an older person (as I am), your hearing is probably not as acute as it once was, and you may have the early stages of glaucoma leaving you with lousy peripheral vision. These have no impact when you are watching TV with the sound turned up or reading a book. These may have an adverse impact, however, if you are employed in a retail setting. A customer waving and calling out to get your attention unsuccessfully may assume that you are rude and uncaring. It wouldn't occur to him that you just didn't see or hear him. You are not *disabled* – you can still see and hear – just not as well as you once could.

A person with autism may have excellent vision and hearing, but may be unable to comfortably make eye contact. Will he do well in the retail setting where customers will be calling on him for help? Possibly, but he'll really have to work at it.

46

The clients we served at Merrick were evaluated on a regular basis in a number of areas – physical skills (strength, manual dexterity), cognitive skills (ability to process information, acquire knowledge, solve problems), and social skills (social perceptiveness, ability to interact with others). They were encouraged to work on any shortcomings that <u>they</u> perceived as hindrances to their own personal development.

Many of our clients worked out in the community, both individually and on work crews. They held retail and restaurant jobs, worked on cleaning crews, and performed clerical work. Many others worked at our facility in areas specifically set up to facilitate production work and social interactions – both client-to-client and client-to-staff. Most of the work performed in our building was light assembly and packaging jobs, shredding documents, and recycling; all jobs performed under contracts for third parties. We also hired our own clients for janitorial work and van washing. The whole idea was to find or create jobs that the clients <u>could</u> do, and <u>wanted</u> to do.

Most of the work was manual, but even the most fundamental steps require some cognitive processing. Each job was broken into discreet steps in a process called *task analysis*. Here's an example of a simple kitting job:

1. place label on a zip-lock bag
2. count out ten items
3. pour into the bag and zip the bag closed
4. weigh the bag to insure the right count
5. place completed kits in box
6. weigh box to insure the right count
7. tape the box closed and label

A job like this could be accomplished by a client or two. But we would often assign work like this to a team of eight clients plus a job coach, with the clients selected for specific tasks based on their skill sets and abilities. The whole idea was to create meaningful work for as many people as possible.

Some say it is hard to have a great life unless it is a meaningful life, and difficult to have a meaningful life without meaningful work.

--John Wayne Barker

None of our clients at Merrick really had to work. They lived with their families or in group homes. Food, clothing, and shelter were provided. They worked because they wanted their own spending money, and when payday rolled around every two weeks, it was A REALLY BIG DEAL!

A lot of the clients took great pride in showing off their paychecks. And there was more to it than the numbers on the check and the buying power that represented. They took pride in *earning* the paycheck, and not having it given to them like a weekly allowance.

Work for people who are economically disadvantaged

In the book *Scarcity, Why Having Too Little Matters So Much*, Sendhil Mullainathan and Eldar Shafir present an insightful study on the way we behave during periods of scarcity. Much of their book is focused on a scarcity of income – having too little money to meet the basic needs of a household. Many of us are quick to assume that those living in poverty *are poor precisely because they are less capable.* The authors counter:

> *Our data suggest causality runs at least as strongly in the other direction: that poverty—the scarcity mindset— causes failure.*[31]

Those living in poverty cannot help but be obsessed with their dire financial situation, and in that state of mind, have difficulty maintaining attention on other things that directly impact their family's lives: being fully engaged at work, ensuring kids are behaving and learning in school, making sure doctor's appointments are kept, etc.

Another way to think about this is through the lens of Maslow's 5-level hierarchy of human needs. Maslow maintained that we need to satisfy lower-level needs before we can think about tackling those above. Those living in poverty are struggling with food-clothing-shelter issues. With that mindset, it's hard to focus on anything higher on the pyramid, including safety issues, which could certainly have an adverse 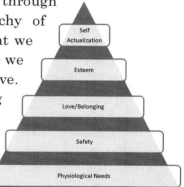 impact on their duties at work. Given this, is it any wonder that very poor individuals have a hard time being effective employees?

Employers are not parents. We no longer expect the sort of paternalistic relations Disraeli referred to in Trafford's factory town. But it certainly wouldn't hurt employers to be aware of their employees' mindset when they come to work in the morning. What employers surely <u>should</u> do is pay their employees enough to lift them out of poverty! They may find, to their delight, that they have a much stronger workforce than they first assumed.

Part time work for students

By the time children reach high school, a lot of them get the *opportunity* to work part time and earn a little of their own money. This is a good thing, an important part of their education. First, they will learn quite quickly that the *fun* part of working that they all fascinated about as preschoolers may have been overestimated just a bit. In a delightful column titled *Take it from teacher: Johnny needs a job*, Gina Barreca spells out how having a real job can make young adults better students. Whether baby-sitting, mowing grass, or shoveling snow for another family (not at home – not a chore), working food service, retail, warehouse, movie theatre; any paid employment; all these can help make better students. How so?

> *They'll wake up at a scheduled time and get their acts together in order to show up for work before their shift begins while wearing neither clothes nor an expression that looks as if it just emerged from a laundry basket.*

> *They'll learn that they are not the only important people in the room and that the world isn't intrigued by their drama. They'll learn cooperation, teamwork, time management and what it's like to fall asleep as soon as their head hits the pillow at the end of a long day.*

> *Young people who have held jobs are better students because they know they can't do everything at the last minute, all at once or erratically.*

> *They should get a grip on taxes and Social Security, open a checking account in their own name and have a certain amount of autonomy over spending what they earn. They will then learn what things cost by purchasing them with their own dough.* [32]

All of these traits make better students. They also make better citizens.

Special minimum wage

The Department of Labor allows companies to pay adults with disabilities special minimum wages which are lower than the standard minimum wage. The policy is tightly regulated by DOL, with the special wage based on the productivity of a disabled person compared to that of a "qualified, experienced worker", taking normal breaks and fatigue factors into account.

The justification for this policy is that many adults with disabilities are unable to produce work at the same pace as able-bodied workers, and paying them proportionately lower wages is fair for both parties. The policy is meant both to encourage companies to hire adults with disabilities in spite of their lower productivity rates, and to give those adults a chance to work and to feel the pride of earning a paycheck.

The special minimum wage, which at first blush seems heartless, is actually a pretty good policy. Without it, many adults with disabilities would not be able to find any meaningful work.

The rationale for special minimum wages could apply to students with part time jobs. Many students, in their own way, have a disability when it comes to work. It's called being a teenager! When they go in to work and are assigned a task, that task may not command the center of their attention. They have other, more important things to deal with.

I'm not being sarcastic here. Teenagers really do have more important things to deal with than working. There is school – academics, art, music, and athletics. And there's that raging-hormone thing – sorting out boy-girl relationships, sexual identities, family and community responsibilities, and generational roles. How to be a good worker fits in there somewhere, but it's not front-of-mind for most teenagers. But as Ms. Barreca tells us, *Johnny needs a job*, so allowing companies to pay special minimum wages to students will give employers the incentive for doing so.

Some of the arguments against raising the minimum wage zero in on high school and college students holding down part time jobs. The argument goes like this: 1) they're not worth it – they don't work as hard as my older employees, they're just not as conscientious, and 2) they don't need it – they come from middle class families and they have part time jobs just for the spending money, not to support a family. Whether or not these have any validity, if we take these arguments away from opponents of higher wages for workers, it may make it easier for those employers to accept higher pay for adults who are responsible for supporting themselves and trying to raise a family.

Perhaps the easiest way to do this would be to have a two-tiered minimum wage – with a lower tier that applies to those under 21 years of age, and the higher standard minimum wage that applies to those 21 and older. The rationale for doing this is to encourage companies to hire younger workers on a part time basis. The justification is twofold: First, because a fair number of these student/workers are less conscientious than many of their older counterparts who are in the position of supporting themselves, it is fair for employers to pay them less. And second, we want student/workers to be students first. The lessons they are learning on the job are an extension of those being learned in school.

The importance of work

The first lesson learned is that work is important. Work is what we do to earn a paycheck – our labor in exchange for compensation. We learn that the labor market is the mechanism humans have invented to ensure that work gets done, that we survive individually, and thrive as a species.

Work is important to all of us, both socially and economically. Reading from Ryan Avent's *The Wealth of Humans, Work, Power, and Status in the Twenty-first Century*:

> *Most of us now of working age ... inherited an idea of work ... as a positive good: economically necessary and morally beneficial. When work works, we understood, it provides a basis for a stable social order. It gives people something to do. It gives workers the sense that they are contributing to society and to the welfare of their families.* [33]

In Richard Florida's book called *The Rise of the Creative Class* [34], he breaks the labor force into three classes: the Creative Class, the Working Class, and the Service Class. The creative class are those individuals fortune has smiled on. Through their talent, their intelligence, their hard work, and of course through their family connections, they have good jobs, are performing meaningful work, and have handsome compensation packages. These are, for the most part, upper and upper-middle income class families. The creative class is on the rise (33% the workforce now, 14% 80 years ago), good news because all of us should aspire to reach this status. Mr. Florida's working class (largely factory and construction workers) is shrinking (23% now, down from 54% in 1930), and that's too bad for us economically because these were well-paid jobs. Florida's service class is growing rapidly (46% now, up from 30% in 1930), and is taking up some of the slack from the working class. This is a mixed bag of good and bad economic news. Some of these jobs are very well-paid, but for many, Florida writes

> *At its minimum-wage worst, life in the Service Class is a grueling struggle for subsistence amid the wealth of others.*

David Brooks has some fun with the creative class in a book called *Bobos in Paradise*[35]. Bobos being short for bourgeois and bohemian. It used to be that a bourgeoisie businessman in a gray flannel suit was a distinctly different character from a bohemian artist. Brooks contends that they have much more in common than they'd like to admit.

Authors Barbara Ehrenreich and David Shipler look at life at the other end of the workforce spectrum, Ehrenreich with *Nickel and Dimed*[36] and Shipler with *The Working Poor*[37] Working for short stints in service sector jobs herself, Ehrenreich introduces us to several of her co-workers. They are subjected to irregular hours, shitty bosses, and tiny paychecks. They cannot work their way up the economic ladder, not because they don't have the talent, but because they are stuck in impossible predicaments, at work and at home, that keep them locked in the lower class. Shipler interviewed dozens of low-income workers from coast to coast, some over the course of five or six years. This allowed him to compare their lives during periods of economic boom and bust, and see that either way, many are trapped in their condition of poverty.

But I don't mean to dwell on class warfare at this point of the book. (I'll save that for Chapters 8-10.) What I want to stress here is that work is important to <u>all</u> of us: whether members of the *Creative Class* or *Bobos in Paradise*, or working stiffs from *Nickel and Dimed* and from the pages of Studs Terkel's *Working*. Work is as important to me as to my neighbor, and as important to the baker in Boston as to the breadwinner in Bangalore. It is universally true – work is important to all of us. So much so, that the work we do becomes a part of our very identity.

I've talked a lot about the in-service aspect of work. That virtue was not lost with the advent of working to create personal wealth. We see workers in every sector of the economy who earn relatively modest wages but experience great satisfaction on the job. They obviously find their work meaningful and fulfilling, modest paychecks notwithstanding.

So, crazy as it sounds, we should all work less! That way there will be enough work to go around for all of us to share. The joy that many experience at work will not diminish when the workweek is shrunk from five to three days. Quite the contrary. Understanding that work is as precious to my neighbor as it is to me will make it easier to share the number of hours of paid work hours available to all of us.

But we seem to have a problem with sharing, a topic we'll cover in the next chapter.

CHAPTER 3

The Drive for Wealth

THE OBJECTIVE OF THIS CHAPTER is to explain why we are still working 40 hours a week instead of closing in on the 15-hour a workweek John Maynard Keynes predicted. In the last chapter, we learned that our very identity is tied to our careers, that *we are what we do*. In this chapter, we'll see how our identity is also closely tied to material measures of wealth, that *we are what we own*.

First, a little background. Contrary to popular belief, consumerism wasn't an invention of Madison Avenue. (They just reduced it to an art by applying scientific measurement to the efficacy of advertising and other promotional campaigns.) Most likely, the psychological drive to 'keep up with the Joneses' predates even the agrarian age. We can imagine hunter/gatherer clans comparing their shiny baubles with those of neighboring clans. When they saw something they liked, you can bet they had to have it. And have it they would – either by force (when at war and raiding enemy camps), or by trade (during peaceful periods).

Indeed, it was probably material objects that one group had and the other wanted that precipitated many of the interactions between one tribe and another in the first place. The two opposing tribes had to figure out if they were better off when these interactions were the result of peaceful trade, or the spoils of belligerent acts of war.

War or peace, it would have been hard for any of these tribes to possess a <u>lot</u> of material things because they were nomadic people. Certain tools and shelters were surely carried from one campsite to the next – much easier to do that than to start off from scratch. And those nomadic clans would also have carried along some objects that seemingly had no utilitarian value, *baubles unnecessary for anything other than prestige.* (Methinks Madonna, our favorite *Material Girl,* has had kindred sisters for a long, long time.)

About 12,000 years ago, when we advanced from the hunter/gatherer stage to the age of agriculture, we moved from a nomadic lifestyle to living in permanent settlements. At that point, the opportunity to "own" things really kicked into gear because now we didn't have to lug everything along on our nomadic journeys. With portability constraints on possessions removed, consumers could now amass a greater number of things and a much higher volume of man-made goods. The level of consumption of material goods became an increasingly important factor in the economies of communities.

Let's imagine a scenario in 10,000 BC where our family became very good over time at gathering firewood – specializing in cutting, drying and bundling the firewood into neat transportable packets. Meanwhile, our friendly neighbors became very good at raising pigs. We would make excess bundles of firewood with the intention of supplying them to our neighbor in exchange for some of his piglets. We would count on our neighbor to supply us with pigs because he needed our firewood. Without our neighbor's demand for our firewood, and our demand for his pigs, he'd often be cold, and we'd often be hungry.

If trade were limited to our two households, it's unlikely that we'd ever produce more firewood than that needed by our little enclave of two families. But at some point, our two families started to bring firewood and piglets into the market in town.

We then spent even more time in the woods, at <u>work</u>, so we'd have more bundles of wood available to bring to the market for trade. At the same time, our neighbors worked even harder to raise more pigs. The surplus material we created could be used to trade for a variety of provisions that could be found in town, a vastly greater variety than the two commodities we had been limited to. At that point, the market economy was born, with Consumers of goods just as critical to the whole process as the Producers.

Market induced greed

When our family and the neighbors showed up at the market with our firewood and our piglets, we'd find more families and a host of other products available for barter: food, clothing, tools, cooking utensils. (No Pet Rocks yet.) All the traders wanted a piece of the action, and there certainly would have been stiff competition between the different vendors, with the winners being those who could structure the best deals and get the best value in exchange for their own product and service offerings.

Eventually, money came along as a handy way to keep track of transactions, and the market now had a convenient way of keeping score. Money also eliminated the physical limitations of the accumulating wealth. (Back when the unit of exchange was a bag of wheat, there was only so much one could accumulate before the oldest grain began to rot away.)

With the physical and temporal constraints removed, is it possible that these earliest market traders were just as guilty of greed and avarice as we are today? Did the firewood bundler spend hours in the woods that should have been spent back home with the wife and kids? Did the pig farmer raise so many animals his whole farm reeked? In an obsessive drive to obtain more wealth, is it also possible that our two families were never entirely satisfied with the things they've acquired from the market?

Each subsequent generation of these prehistoric traders would probably be better off materially than the last. Would they be happier? Maybe not. All of that is just conjecture of course, since we have nothing written down.

Once we did start writing things down, we find plenty of evidence that wealth does not equal happiness.

Browsing on the internet, I was able to find these quotes on the impact of greed and avarice going all the way back to classical times:

- *He who is content with what he has would not be content with what he would like to have.* Socrates[1]
- *An object in possession seldom retains the charm it held in pursuit.* Pliny the Elder[1]
- *Some men make fortunes not to enjoy them; for, blinded by avarice, they live to make fortunes.* Juvenal[2]

Leaping way ahead to 19th century Europe and America:

- *Most men pursue pleasure with such haste that they hurry past it.* Kiekegaard[1]
- *It is the preoccupation with possessions, more than anything else, that prevents us from living freely and nobly.* Thoreau[1]
- *It is one of the worst effects of prosperity to make a man a vortex instead of a fountain; so that, instead of throwing out, he learns only to draw in.* Henry Ward Beecher[2]
- *Possessions are usually diminished by possession.* Nietzche[1]

And finally, to today:

- *Traditionally, too much wealth, too much materialism, was understood to impede human progress, leading to greed and envy (twin sins that feed on each other), luxury, indolence, and the slavery of selfishness.* Benjamin Hunnicutt
- *Money alone cannot buy pleasure, though it can help. For enjoyment is an art and a skill for which we have little talent or energy.* Alan Watts
- *Don't get so busy making a living that you forget to make a life.* Dolly Parton
- *I'd even bitch if I was getting hung with a gold rope.* Susan Barghini
- *I will never be satisfied with my collection of quotes on greed.* John Crea

[1]www.tentmaker.org/quotes.greedquotes.html
[2]www.bartelby.com/348/114.html

Henry David Thoreau was acutely aware of this phenomenon, and lived his life accordingly. In 1854, he gives us this observation in *Walden, or, Life in the Woods*:

> But men labor under a mistake. The better part of the man is soon plowed into the soil for compost. By a seeming fate, commonly called necessity, they are employed, as it says in the old book, laying up treasures that moth and rust will corrupt and thieves will break through and steal. It is a fool's life, as they will find when they get to the end of it, if not before.[38]

One hundred sixty years after Thoreau penned that dreary passage, John Cleese, one of the creative, comic geniuses behind *Monty Python's Flying Circus*, is quoted in a column by Lee Schafer in the StarTribune:

(Cleese) explained that he was currently puzzling over what to make of another serious subject, of why already wealthy people seem grimly determined to accumulate a lot more money. "I'd love to do a TV series on that," he said. "I would love to talk to such people and say 'Why do you need so much money?' And why do people say it is so admirable? I think the world has gone quite mad."[39]

I believe Mr. Cleese is quite right. But let me play devil's advocate here: The corrupting nature of greed notwithstanding, there is no denying the overall benefit to mankind of commercial markets driven by the profit motive. Consider indices of immutable progress: lower infant mortality rates, longer life expectancies, greater creature comforts, and the evolution of social institutions. We are all immeasurably healthier and wealthier than we were generations ago. It is the interactions of buyers and sellers in open markets, *competitive capitalism*, that can take a fair amount of credit for this progress. That said, those interactions have become cold and calculated economic exchanges.

The lost connection between producers and consumers

We are social animals. Our hunter/gatherer ancestors had clear knowledge about which members of the clan were most productive: who were the bravest hunters, who were most clever at gathering nuts, who made the best stone tools. Throughout most of the agricultural era, everyone in town knew the firewood

The invisible hand of the market was quite visible when the buyers and sellers of goods knew each other personally.

bundler and the pig farmer. Moving ahead to the middle ages, when you bought a pair of shoes, you weren't just buying a pair of fine leather brogans; you were buying the efforts and artistry of the cobbler. For the great majority of our two million years of tenure here on earth, there was a very personal connection between producers and consumers of goods.

THAT ALL CHANGED with the onset of the industrial age.

There is a neat essay that was written back in 1958 titled: *I, Pencil: My Family Tree as told to Leonard E. Read*[40]. It shows us just how far we have come from those simpler times when you knew the cobbler by name (Schumacher, of course). Although I disagree with the ultimate conclusions Mr. Read draws regarding the superiority of laissez-faire markets, his description of the modern (1958) manufacturing process is illustrative. Read tells us about the thousands of people who play a role in making the simple wooden pencil that your kindergartener uses to trace letters and numbers.

> *I Pencil* starts out life as a cedar tree in Oregon. That tree is chopped down by a lumberjack who may have been amazed to learn that part of the tree he just fell will end up being used to make pencils.

> *I, Pencil's* lead is no longer made from the element lead, of course. It turns out to be a mixture of graphite from Sri Lanka (Ceylon in 1958) and clay from Mississippi. Miners of those specialty materials may or may not know that their minerals will end up in pencils. But we can be sure they don't know who ultimately buys these writing instruments.

Read's essay, thorough as it is, does not include the thousands of people who get involved after the manufacturing process with the distribution and the sale of *I, Pencil*. The people responsible for selling pencils know all about you and your children quite well <u>as customers</u>; but they don't know <u>you</u> from Adam.

This ignorance works both ways. While you have a brief encounter with the checkout person at the store where you bought the pencils, you certainly have no exchange whatsoever with the lumberjack from Oregon, with the graphite miner from Sri Lanka, or anyone else in *I, Pencil's* provenance. You might <u>like</u> to know them – you might find them to be interesting and delightful people. But there is no opportunity to do so. Trading in the market today is a purely an economic exchange – my dollars for your products. There is no interaction between the producer and the consumer of commercial goods. No verbal exchange between pig farmer and firewood gatherer.

WITHOUT A PERSONAL CONNECTION to the people who make the products we buy, our reasons for selecting one brand over another, and one store or another, are limited to <u>our perceptions</u> of convenience, price, quality, and prestige. (Our perceptions are highly influenced by folks who earn their living in advertising.)

The fact is, most of us are pretty shallow individuals when it comes to consuming goods and services. We are happy to let someone else tell us what to buy, when to buy, and what brand to buy. We care little for the social consequences of our purchase, and are much more concerned with whether or not we got a good deal. (This is not really meant to be a criticism. Just an observation.)

Natural resource constraints on consumption
If money eliminated the problem of needing enough space to hold

our wealth, it did not remove the physical constraints on production that are imposed by a limited amount of raw material and energy available to create the products and services in the first place.

Today we consume natural resources as fast as we can pump them out of the ground, dig them out of a mountain, clear-cut them from a forest, and harvest them from a field. Relatively few of us are employed in primary extraction industries and farming. More of us work in manufacturing and food processing (although this number is shrinking as factories become more automated). More yet in the distribution of goods to the end-user (this includes retail establishments). But all of us are 'employed' as consumers of these goods. Upper, middle, and lower-class families all have to eat. All need essential clothing and shelter. Moving from the lower to the middle class, families become prodigious consumers of natural resources. Thus, as the middle class grows around the world, so does the consumption of these resources.

Thomas Robert Malthus warned us about the catastrophic problems of a geometrically exploding human population. He predicted that the number of mouths to feed would soon outstrip the amount of food available for consumption. That was in 1798.

We somehow managed to avoid that catastrophe.

Actually, there is no 'somehow' about it. Our good fortune was not by accident. We avoided catastrophe by increasing the amount of food produced per acre at a pace greater than the population growth. It was the impetus of market demand (along with the prospect of getting rich meeting that demand), and the implementation of technological improvements, that made all this possible.

Since the start of the industrial revolution, each time it looked like natural resource constraints would cause the economic underpinnings of our society to become unraveled, the markets found a way to right themselves. Either there were technological developments that resulted in greater production, or we came up with go-arounds – finding substitute products for those now in short supply.

We make use of a potent combination of engineering and marketing skills to address solutions to shortage problems. Packaging of products is a good example. For a while, it seemed like everything you bought consisted of more packaging than product. My personal nemesis – the impossible-to-open blister pack! In some cases, the added packaging was meant to deter theft. In other cases, it provided additional space for advertising and information. (E.g., a thumb drive mounted on a much larger hang-card.) There are flashy, non-recyclable ways of doing this, and there are quieter, more environmentally benign (recyclable) ways of doing the same thing. If consumers insist on the latter, manufacturers will make those changes in packaging. (If we are not passive as consumers, the market will respond.)

In spite of dire warnings from modern-day Malthusians, we always seem to find a way to keep the consumer-based economy going. HOWEVER, that does not mean we can count on technology to bail us out forever. It seems like with each 'crisis', the solutions get a little trickier. And sooner or later, we are going to butt up against a problem that we can't surpass without a great deal of disruption to the status quo.

Global Warming/Climate Change just may be that problem. Most scientists who study these things tell us that the growing levels of carbon in the air will greatly increase the likelihood of a greenhouse effect, with the atmosphere holding more and more heat inside. The results could be catastrophic, with significant changes to the climate worldwide, and with rising sea levels, to the point where we'll lose a lot of low-lying land along the coasts (where millions of humans live).

You may or may not agree with this forecast. But if you think there is even a sliver of a chance that this is true, the conservative approach would be to minimize the amount of carbon we are adding to the atmosphere posthaste. Yet it is the conservatives on the political spectrum who proudly label themselves 'deniers'. Odd.

Especially odd when you think about the potential of all the money to be made finding replacements in the energy market for fossil fuels. If ever there was an opportunity for a market to reinvent itself, and make a lot of people ridiculously wealthy in the process, this is it! (Apparently, some folks are more interested in protecting their conservative investments in coal, oil, & gas than they are in protecting our planet.)

REDUCE – REUSE – RECYCLE. That is the mantra environmentally aware teachers share with their students. They are in that order very intentionally. As far as the environment is concerned, not buying something in the first place is better than buying something that you don't really need, even if it's advertised as 'green' or environmentally friendly. It is not just the responsibility of Producers to build ever-greener products, nor solely the responsibility of the Government to pass laws protecting the environment. Consumers have a responsibility to get by with less, if possible; and when we do need to buy something, we should select products that create the smallest footprint on our planet.

And a note about this – protecting our planet. It's not really our planet that needs protection. Mother Earth is a spry 4.5-billion-year-old orb, made of iron, oxygen, silicon, magnesium, and dozens of other elements, circling the Sun every 365 days.[41] She will shrug off any temporary shift in the climate as easily as the last ice age. It is the inhabitants of the Earth's fragile biosphere who are at risk from climate change, including we frail humans – all of us contributing to the problem in the first place! (I think that's called poetic justice.)

ONE LAST THING to say on this sustainability topic. Shifting to a 24-hour workweek will not have a significant impact on the overall level of natural resources consumed. (The economy will continue to grow, as will the global expansion of the middle class. Both will result in growth in the consumption of goods and services.) But hopefully the shorter workweek will shift our focus from material measures of wealth to other positive experiences that enhance our well-being and are not so resource-dependent. We'll address that more carefully in the next chapter.

The work-consume treadmill

But a shorter workweek is not where we are today. Today we are all about consumption, which means we are all about work. We spend an average of 47 hours per week at work*, just about twice what I am proposing as a standard workweek for a healthy economy and a stronger, sustainable labor market. The reason we are working twice as much as we have to, near as I can tell, is because we are so pre-disposed to increasing the amount of stuff in our possession.

Just like our firewood-gathering and pig-farming ancestors, we put in long hours at work in order to get rich enough to buy all those things we really 'need'.

- First the things we really do need (i.e., the most basic versions of food, clothing, shelter).

---

* The average fulltime job in the U.S. in 2013.

68

- Then upgrades of those basic goods so that we may live in more comfortably.
- Then 'affordable' luxury items (e.g., nicer cars, vacations) that all our neighbors seem to be enjoying.
- Finally, downright opulence. Goods and services that prove that we have shot past the status of reasonably well-off, and we are now able to hang with the truly wealthy.

As we 'ascend' this hierarchy of needs, it seems that our level of wealth will never be sufficient. By the time we reach any one rung on the ladder of consumption, we can be sure that the next rung is calling us higher. So, we double down on our work and continue with our insatiable consumption – spinning away madly on a work/shop treadmill.

Apparently, we never can accumulate enough wealth. Therefore, we can never put in enough hours at work. And sadly, we sometimes forget why we jumped into this rat-race in the first place.[42]

SEVERAL AUTHORS have tackled this subject in the last 25 years, including:

- *Affluenza*[43] by de Graaf, Wann, & Naylor
- *Consumed*[44] by Benjamin Barber
- *Turbo-Capitalism*[45] by Edward Luttwak
- *The Geography of Nowhere*[46] by James Kunstler

The approach of some of these books is to attack the 'system', the sales and marketing departments of large international corporations that lead us down this path of folly. They are right, but only to a point. We are not forced into the Target or Walmart store by gunpoint. We follow the lead of the advertisers gladly, just as eager for the newest shiny bauble as the next guy.

Consumers of goods have little regard for producers, even though they spend their days at work producing goods and services themselves. We have forgotten a large part of what all the work is for. Namely, the benefits to the larger community. We have no personal connections to the producers of goods, so we see none of the consequences of our purchases on their well-being. With the services we purchase, there is a bit more of a connection. But most often the personal connection is strictly professional, perfunctory. How can we be in the 'good citizen' mode when we are driven solely by selfish consumption?

But in spite of all the mindless consumption, this has proven to be a good thing for modern man collectively, raising the standard of living for 7 billion souls worldwide. We are living longer, healthier, and in far more comfort than our ancestors. Poverty rates are rapidly shrinking worldwide. It has even had an impact on warfare, as there is less chance two countries will go to war with each other when they are busy negotiating trade agreements. In toto, life is better for the vast majority of us.

Comparative wealth

Wealth is a peculiar concept. Quite relative in one sense, absolute in another. Relative because we constantly compare ourselves with our immediate peers – siblings, classmates, neighbors. Absolute because all of us, at one time or another, gaze with secret envy at the *Lifestyles of the Rich and Famous*.

Columnist George Will talked about comparative wealth in an essay. He referred to the 'positional economy' as a place where you and I are constantly comparing our social status based on the consumption of goods and services. Talking about ostentatious consumption (like $12 cups of coffee at Starbucks), he wrote:

> *After elementary needs – food, shelter, clothing – are satisfied, consumption nevertheless continues, indeed it intensifies because desires are potentially infinite. People compare themselves to their neighbors, envy their neighbors' advantages, and strive to vault ahead in the envy-ostentation sweepstakes.*

Will goes on to write:

> *Where will the positional economy end? It won't. Stanford professor Francis Fukuyama notes that it is a peculiarity of human beings that they desire some things "not for themselves but because they are desired by other human beings." Hamsters have more sense. This characteristic of our species – the quest for recognition by distinguishing oneself from others – provides limitless marketing possibilities because for many wealthy people, "the chief enjoyment of riches consists in the parade of riches." So wrote Adam Smith in "The Wealth of Nations," published in the resonant year of 1776.*[47]

GEOGRAPHICALLY, we also see comparisons of wealth that are simultaneously relative and absolute. Poor families in the U.S. and Europe are absolutely better off than poor families in parts of Africa and Asia. But the poor in the wealthier countries don't think of themselves as well-off. They see themselves as poor because, relatively speaking, within their own countries, they are!

For middle class Americans and Europeans, it seems like we are never satisfied with our comfortable homes, our working cars, and our enjoyable vacation trips. We are always comparing ourselves to those better off than we are. And the only way we can increase our level of consumption is to put in more time at work and earn bigger paychecks.

We are all born with a competitive spirit (E.O. Wilson's *part sinner*). This is manifested in what we do and what we own. It is only natural for us to want to possess things – a lot of things – the very best of things. (Certainly, better than yours!)

The competition for status, through the things we own and the services we consume, is apparently something that can never be fully satisfied. This keeps the labor market humming and the GDP growing, and that is great for everyone......... until it isn't anymore.

CHAPTER 4

Leisure Time Lost

IN THE LAST CHAPTER, we learned how our incessant drive to consume goods and services has resulted in economic growth. Now, we need to channel some of that competitive spirit toward the amount of leisure time at our disposal. A 24-hour workweek will result in 16 extra hours of free time for each fulltime worker to spend on activities of their choice (the definition of leisure time). I am proposing that this will be mandated for hourly workers, not for those on salaries. But, we can be quite sure, there will be a trickle-up effect.

It will not take long for all the salaried men and women who are putting in 60+ hours a week at work to sit up and take notice. Will salaried workers drop their hours all the way down to 24? Probably not. My guess is that they'll probably dial their workweek back to something closer to 40-hours/week. Still one helluva gain in leisure time, time available to spend with their families.

Placing a value on leisure time

It's easy enough to place a monetary value on all the goods and services we consume because they come with a price tag attached: a $5 happy meal, a $50 massage, a $500 mattress. But how does one quantify the value of an hour of leisure?

Economists address this question with a concept called *Labor Supply*, and they spell out all the factors that enter into the labor supply decisions that we make. George Borjas, in his textbook *Labor Economics*, writes

> *individuals seek to maximize their well-being by consuming goods (such as fancy cars and nice homes) and leisure. Goods have to be purchased in the marketplace. Because most of us are not independently wealthy, we must work in order to earn the cash required to buy the desired goods. The economic tradeoff is clear: If we do not work, we can consume a lot of leisure, but we have to do without the goods and services that make life more enjoyable. If we do work, we will be able to afford many of these goods and services, but we must give up some of our valuable leisure time.* [48]

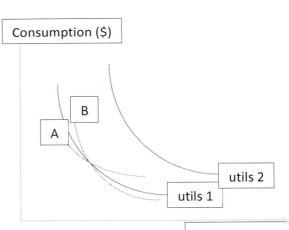

Economists model this Utility Function: $U = f(C, L)$; and they draw nice, neat *Indifference Curves* where every combination of C (the consumption of goods and services) and L (the consumption of leisure) add up to an equal number of *utils* [utils 1] Higher curves equal greater numbers of *utils* [utils 2], which denotes a happier worker/consumer. A flatter curve denotes a worker who values consumption more than leisure [A]. A steeper curve just the opposite [B].

All this looks great on paper, and it is a good way to look at the tradeoffs. But seldom, in real life, are such tradeoffs available to the worker.

If you are a fulltime hourly worker, you <u>will</u> put in your 40 hours/week. If you are salaried, you are <u>expected</u> to work 50 – 60 hours a week, just like everyone else. The only ones who have the freedom to work as many or as few hours as they choose are those who have already achieved some level of financial independence. That tends to be the *golden-agers* who have been fortunate enough to have had good jobs for most of their working lives and are now able to live in some comfort on their retirement savings.

This brings up a good point. At different stages of our life, the slope of our personal Indifference Curves will look much different. Parents with pre-school children will need to spend more time at home. (Note that I said parents, not mothers.) Those with school age children will want to spend more time at work, saving up for the kids' college expenses. Empty nesters may choose more work, saving for their own retirement, or less, all dependent of their financial comfort level.

As a retired person, I often have the distinct pleasure of being on Grandpa-duty. That includes walking the younger kids to and from school. It's an easy 15-minute walk that I enjoy, and it is certainly good for both me and the kids. So, we walk whenever we can, only resorting to the car when the weather turns truly brutish (which happens too often during our Minnesota winters).

When I first started walking the kids to school, I was dismayed by all the parents who drove their kids, even on the nicest days. I know most of these families live right in the neighborhood. Why weren't they walking? Then it dawned on me. The reason the parents drive is not because they are lazy and don't care about their children's health. They drive because they don't have time to take an hour out of their day (1/2 hour before and after school) because they have to work too damn much! Consequently, every morning and every afternoon, in fair weather and foul, there is a long queue of cars in front of the school.

Our grandkids go to the neighborhood public school where they and most of their classmates are from working-class families. As it happens, there is also a very prestigious private school in the neighborhood where, one assumes, most of the students are from higher-income families with parents in the professions. Well, just like the public school, they have a long queue of cars dropping off and picking up kids each day. The cars may be newer and nicer, but those parents don't have time to carve an hour out of their day to walk with their kids to school either.

ECONOMISTS AGREE that an hour of leisure is a good, just like a product or a service we consume. But placing a value on an hour of leisure is not an easy task. How do you compare the value of an hour of free time for the CEO to that for a janitor? The CEO is paid 400 times more than the janitor. Does that mean his free time is worth 400 times more? If that's true, they sure don't act like it (consider Yahoo's CEO Marissa Meyer claiming a 130-hour workweek). If fact, in many respects, high level execs and business owners are <u>always</u> at work, never truly 'off the clock'.

The janitor, on the other hand, doesn't fret about work when he goes home, and he puts in zero extra hours voluntarily, punching in and out of his 40-hour job precisely on time. Of course, he's probably punching in and out of two 40-hour jobs because he can't afford to feed his family on just one. An 80-hour workweek leaves the janitor with just 32 hours of leisure per week (after subtracting out 8 hours a day for sleep). So from a scarcity perspective, a single hour of leisure time may now be worth more to the janitor than the CEO.

And then there's the quality of an hour of leisure consumed. The CEO is wealthy enough to hire someone else to cut the grass, cook the meals, even nanny the kids; or he can choose to do those duties himself when he finally gets home. The janitor has no choice in the matter. If there is snow that needs to be shoveled, he grabs his boots and jacket.

With all the chores out of the way, is an additional hour of leisure spent *productively* – say at a concert, or a lecture, or perhaps with a good book (like this one)? Or is the hour of leisure *wasted* at the bar watching a football game?

We should be careful how we judge! If the CEO is still mentally 'on the clock' while he's at the opera, that hour of refined entertainment may have relatively little value to him personally. If the janitor gets to share a rare hour of free time with his equally hard-working wife, and they decide that the best way to do this is to go to the bar and watch the game, that hour surely has a great deal of value to both of them.

While the qualitative attributes of leisure are not easily measured, the overall amount of free time certainly is directly correlated to a worker's well-being. We'll come back to that a little later in this chapter.

Attitudes toward leisure time

Benjamin Hunnicutt has studied the importance of leisure time his entire career. His great book *Free Time,* subtitled *The Forgotten American Dream*, is a historical study of America's attitudes toward leisure time. Hunnicutt takes us all the way back to our nation's founders, and the list of inalienable rights spelled out in the Declaration of Independence – *life, liberty, and the pursuit of happiness.* What did Jefferson and his compatriots mean by that last phrase, *the pursuit of happiness*? What would make us truly happy? In Hunnicutt's words:

> *Where do we go when we have done all our chores, performed our duties, and met our responsibilities? What kinds of human activities or states of being lay beyond social responsibilities and material necessity and are worthwhile in and for themselves?*[49]

Jefferson was a renaissance man. He would've had no problem occupying his leisure time with worthwhile pursuits. The assumption is that other gentlemen would've been equally appreciative of having more time at their disposal.

Leaping ahead about 180 years, John Maynard Keynes shed some light on the meaning of *the pursuit of happiness*, saying that at some point, our time would become more valuable to us than new goods and services. Hunnicutt summarizes Keynes' thoughts on leisure:

> *Then we would welcome the opportunity to live more of our lives outside the marketplace. No longer preoccupied with economic concerns, we could begin to develop our potential to live together peacefully and agreeably, spending more of our time and energy forming healthy families, neighborhoods, and cities; increasing our knowledge and appreciation of nature, history, and other peoples; freely investigating and delighting in the mysteries of the human spirit; exploring our beliefs and values together; finding common ground for agreement and conviviality; living virtuous lives; practicing our faiths; expanding our awareness of God; and wondering in Creation.*[50]

78

Keynes, we must acknowledge, is the economist who predicted that technological development and huge increases in productivity that were evident in the 1930's would allow us to be working about 15 hours a week within 100 years (just 15 years from now). I believe he was on the right track. I think his timing was just off a bit. What happened? The consumer society

A calm and modest life brings more happiness than the pursuit of success combined with constant recklessness.

-Albert Einstein, 1922

happened (see Chapter 3). We live in a world where everyone wants to be wealthy, and the capitalist movers and shakers keep moving the bar as to what constitutes wealth.

RECALL that with the onset of the industrial age, there was a need to keep the capital-intensive factories running as long as possible. Factory owners, given their choice, would keep the men, women, and children laborers on the job around the clock if they could.

Eventually, political pressure was brought to bear, and the government stepped up and provided some relief for the workers. This started with child labor laws early in the 1800's in England. From then on, there was a persistent, if unsteady, push for worker protection in Europe and North America. Factory workers were required to put in 12 – 18 hour days, six days a week early in the industrial revolution. This was pared down to 10-hour days, five and a half days a week in the 1840's, and to an 8-hour day as early as 1877, following an executive order by President Grant covering manual laborers under government contracts.

The push for shorter workdays continued all the way up to the Great Depression. For some economists and political leaders, the two primary reasons for the push for shorter workdays at that time had little to do with individual worker welfare. The reasons were macro-economic:

1. The shorter workweek would reduce levels of unemployment.
2. Increased leisure time would accelerate consumer demand.

But there were qualitative reasons as well, namely that more leisure time has significance beyond its simple economic value (as spelled out earlier in the comments from Keynes). There were those who thought work should become *decentered, made subordinate to the more important business of living.*[51] (Hunnicutt)

Many jobs had become so narrow, so mechanized, so paced by the assembly line, that it is easy to see why there was such a push to work shorter hours. Labor leaders in the 1920's were arguing that mechanization and industrial efficiency made both higher wages and shorter hours possible.

But with the onset of the Great Depression, which preceded the stock market crash of 1929 by a few months, came massive unemployment rates in virtually every industry. Suddenly, the idea of spending less time at work had very little to do with the beneficial improvement of workers' lives. Not working meant being unemployed.

Shorter workdays and working fewer hours a week became the antidote for unemployment. Job sharing became the prime economic mover. Hunnicutt writes:

> *During their conventions in 1932, both parties incorporated work-sharing planks in their platforms and*

then actively campaigned on the issue, Hoover and Roosevelt each claiming to be the original and stronger advocate of the measure.[52]

Many proponents were arguing for a 30-hour workweek at that time. That obviously didn't happen. What did happen to the push for a shorter workweek? It's a bit of a mystery. Hunnicutt indicates that the two parties disagreed with the best way to achieve this shared objective, the Democrats opting for mandated regulation, the Republicans insisting on voluntary measures. (If that did happen, it's just one more case of partisan politics getting in the way of human progress.) At any rate, 1933 would prove to be the *high-water mark* for the *century-long shorter-hours movement.*[53] (Hunnicutt)

Passage of the Fair Labor Standards Act in 1938 would codify the 40-hour workweek. With that, 40-hours became the de facto standard all over the world. And we've been stuck at that mark ever since.

The lost drive for more leisure

In 2016, the Economic Policy Institute responded to the fact that wages have stagnated for the past 35 years, with an 11-point policy proposal they call the *Agenda to Raise America's Pay*:

1. Raise the minimum wage
2. Update overtime rules
3. Strengthen collective bargaining rights
4. Regularize undocumented workers
5. Provide earned sick leave and paid family leave
6. End discriminatory practices that contribute to race and gender inequalities
7. Support strong enforcement of labor standards

8. Prioritize very low rates of unemployment when making monetary policy
9. Enact targeted employment programs and undertake public investments in infrastructure to create jobs
10. Reduce our trade deficit by stopping destructive currency manipulation
11. Use the tax code to restrain top 1% incomes[54]

Only the second and the fifth policies deal with the amount of time a worker puts in on the job. I am surprised that the enlightened, left-leaning economists at EPI have not pushed to reward workers for all the growth in productivity with a shorter workweek and a corresponding increase in free time to spend with their families.

In a 2016 study that Citi GPS co-authored with the Oxford Martin School, a team of analysts are beginning to consider that option. They ask

> *could the 40-hour week (traditionally worked between 9am and 5pm) be coming to an end? … With the rapid increase in automation and technology, could it be that the working hour week would reduce even further when some of our work tasks become automated? Could Keynes' theory of working a 15-hour week actually become a reality?*[55]

Many will question the wisdom of pushing for a shorter workweek. They will remind us of the adage *idle hands are the devil's workshop*, and suggest that if workers are not kept busy on their jobs, they'll be bored with their lives and end up in all sorts of mischief. They will point out that we already don't take all our allotted vacation time, which must mean we want to work more, not less. They will tell us

> *I just can't take the time off – there are things at work that must get done – and I'm the only one qualified to see*

them through.

My response to all of that – *nonsense!*

In a recent column by Professor James Bailey at George Washington University, he tells us that half of all working adults check for work messages at least once a day over the weekend, and the same applies when we finally do go on vacation. He goes on to ask:

> *Certainly, our contributions at work are valuable. But why don't we apply the same thinking to our families? What makes us think our colleagues can't function without us, but our families can?*[56]

The Washington D.C. organization called Project Time Off spells out the personal and productive benefits that are missed when we fail to take time away from work:

- Higher productivity and performance
- More positive attitude toward work
- Increased happiness
- Improved mental and physical health
- Better relationships and social life.[57]

Of course, Project Time Off, like many organizations in the DC area, is a lobbying firm – this particular one working on behalf of the hospitality industry. Not spelled out on their website, but clearly in the interest of their sponsors, are these goals:

- Sell more airline tickets
- Fill more hotel rooms
- Book more restaurant reservations.

This lobbying group quantifies the negative impact on the U.S. economy:

- 658 million vacation days unused (222 million of those simply evaporated because they could not be rolled over)
- $223 billion <u>not</u> pumped into the economy than would've been the case had we fully used our vacation time. (That comes out to over $300 per unused vacation day.)

Their estimate for the negative impact on the economy is suspect. I imagine their assumption is that all 658 M previously unused vacation days would have been spent <u>on a vacation</u>, not hanging around the house, playing with the kids, putzing in the garden, or reading a book.

Retirement 'schedules'

In a 2016 newspaper article by Ginny McReynolds, we learn about how to spend our time in retirement. (Imagine that – the need to learn how to relax!) The article was titled *No longer slaves to the clock, retirees must rethink how to use time.*[58] The article tells us to turn off the alarm clock and ditch the watch. Sleep when you want to sleep, eat when you want to eat, work (on projects of your own choosing) when you want to work, and don't be afraid to relax. There is no need to be tied to an 8-hour day just because that's what you were forced to work when employed. You may still find that 'working' 8-hours a day is just fine, but you may also find that 6 or 4 or 2-hours of work a day on a given project is about right, leaving you more time for other activities. The point is, it's your decision. You no longer need to be a *slave* to the clock.

In a fine book titled *Unretirement*[59], economist Chris Farrell tells how so many of us are taking on new jobs after retirement. We are doing so by our own choice, not because income from the job is necessary for our livelihood. And while we may still need to 'punch in and out', our attitude about this will be far different than when we had no control over our schedules. Back when our paycheck was the only way for us to support our family, if our boss said he needed us on a Sunday morning or a Tuesday evening, we had little choice but to go along. In *unretirement*, we can decide if we want to work those shifts.

Wealth vs. well-being

Measures of wealth and measures of well-being overlap, but are not identical. Most think of wealth as tangible assets: material possessions, money in the bank, owning a business, equity in a home, etc. What is missing? TIME. Time to enjoy the cars and boats you own, the artwork on your walls, the vacation trips you can easily afford but don't take, etc.

Measures of well-being are often less tangible than measures of wealth. That does not make them less important. We can go back to Maslow's pyramid for guidance. It is interesting to look at Well-being and Wealth side-by-side in ascending order of needs:

WELL-BEING	WEALTH
Freedom from hunger and thirst, shelter from the cold	Wealth certainly addresses these needs
Security	One can buy a home in a gated community, a hidden safe, a burglar alarm, and even a security staff. But in a somewhat perverse way, being wealthy makes one <u>less</u> secure. As Willie Sutton reputedly said, he robs banks because that's where the money is.

Affection and affiliation	Enough jokes have been written about sugar-daddies and trophy wives – I don't need to go there.
Esteem	This is where <u>our perception</u> of measures of wealth can really make a difference. If it's prestigious to own a new Chevy, it's even more so to own a new Buick, and better yet to drive a new Cadillac. This relates to our discussion on relative wealth. There is a good chance that your peers, your co-workers, are also putting in 60 – 70 hours a week climbing the corporate ladder to comfortably afford that Cadillac, so it's only natural for you to be doing the same thing.
Self-actualization	If you are putting in 60 – 70 hours a week at work, all in the interest of a larger paycheck, how much time and energy does that leave you for higher-order needs – those more esoteric pursuits that Jefferson and Keynes challenged us to strive for?

If we want to have time for those higher-order needs, we must start putting work back in its place. There is a well-known law of economics called *diminishing marginal utility*. The law states that the marginal utility realized from the consumption of additional units of goods drops with greater numbers. So even though manufacturers and merchants and marketers will tell you that you can never have enough stuff, you can. (In fact, if you live in a three-bedroom rambler, you can sometimes end up with <u>way too much stuff!</u>)

But, know what you can never have enough of? Free time. Even the richest man in the world will tell you he never has time to get everything done. So, do you really want to spend every waking moment on the job just so you can buy more stuff? Or would you rather have a little more time to enjoy all the wonderful things you already have.

Leisure time and creativity

There is a myth of the *starving artist* that suggests that it is <u>need itself</u> that stimulates the creative juices. This falls in with the old adage that *necessity is the mother of invention*. Fred Amram, a professor of creativity and communications at the University of Minnesota, begs to differ. He brings up the opera *La Bohème* by Puccini as an example. The opera makes a great story, but Professor Amram points out the irony that while the Bohemian artists in 1830's Paris were mostly unsuccessful, the composer Puccini was *wealthy and pampered*. Amram wrote:

> *The challenge to the creative person is the problem to be solved, not personal limitations or poverty. Note that the problem for those starving in India has been to grow more rice inexpensively. The solutions, however, come not from India, where farmers live hand-to-mouth – literally. The Indian farmer lacks the leisure to create improved strains of rice. In Minnesota, we have the opportunity to "waste" space by testing diverse crops on the St. Paul campus of the University of Minnesota. We have the "leisure" to do the research that leads to better crops. We have the financial opportunity to pay creative scientists as they invest in new seeds and fertilizing methods. In St. Paul, we solve India's rice problem.* [60]

Amram goes on to describe other instances where the combination of leisure time and available resources lead to creative breakthroughs. The abundance of resources will have a compounding effect – the more leisure – the more creativity.

Tying in with the freedom to explore at universities, 3M has a long-standing R&D policy that allows scientists and engineers to spend up to 15% of their time at work on projects of their own choosing. Their personal projects are often tangential to their primary area of research, and the general idea is that creativity on one will spill over to the other. The corporation is the beneficiary, and the researchers express more satisfaction on the job.

The Ant and the Grasshopper

There is an old fable about an ant and a grasshopper:

> *One bright day in late autumn a family of Ants were bustling about in the warm sunshine, drying out the grain they had stored up during the summer, when a starving Grasshopper, his fiddle under his arm, came up and humbly begged for a bite to eat.*
>
> *"What!" cried the Ants in surprise, "haven't you stored anything away for the winter? What in the world were you doing all last summer?"*
>
> *"I didn't have time to store up any food," whined the Grasshopper; "I was so busy making music that before I knew it the summer was gone."*
>
> *The Ants shrugged their shoulders in disgust. "Making music, were you?" they cried. "Very well; now dance!" And they turned their backs on the Grasshopper and went on with their work.*[61]

The moral of the story: *There's a time for work and a time for play*. And a very famous philosopher reminds us not to forget about the time for play:

---

*All work and no play is a crummy
way to spend your day.
--Curious George*

Summary

The next part of this book focuses on the tremendous productivity gains we have made in the last eighty years. And this begs the question: Why haven't we taken advantage of this progress and allowed ourselves to slow down and act a bit less like the ants? Why, with all the robotic ants we are building, are we not giving ourselves more time to sing and dance like the grasshopper?

The important thing to remember is that leisure time is a *good*, just like the products and services we consume. The impact of an extra hour of leisure time will be greater or less at different times of our lives. But the simple truth is that a greater number of leisure hours will improve our lives and our well-being.

CHAPTER 5

The Impact of Technology and Automation

WHEN I FIRST got the notion to write this book, I assumed the lion's share of my efforts would be devoted to this section. It was 2010, and we were still suffering the aftershocks of the great recession. Unemployment in U.S. was pushing 10%, and was much higher in other places around the world. What seemed clear was that technology and automation had finally (as forecast by many) reached the point where the need for many workers would disappear forever. Several contemporary authors shared this view, notably: Jeremy Rifkin in *The End of Work*[62], Martin Ford in *The Lights in the Tunnel*[63], and Erik Brynjolfsson and Andrew McAfee in *Race Against the Machine*[64]. All voiced deep concern that so many middle class jobs would be permanently eliminated by automation, that consumer demand could not be counted on to keep the economy growing and healthy.

But the labor market, like all markets, is not static, and periodically undergoes significant, even fundamental, changes. It is now early in 2018, and the unemployment rate has fallen steadily to around 4%. And even though we have witnessed a hollowing-out of the middle class, labor demand has once again reacted with more resiliency than expected, and forecasts of doom and gloom have been proven wrong.

That said, there is reason for concern. In Jerry Kaplan's book *Artificial Intelligence*[65], he talks about machines being used not to eliminate entire jobs so much as to perform specific tasks. This results in each worker being more productive, and the need for the number of workers to drop substantially. Robots and automation are eliminating paying jobs in many sectors of the economy at a much faster pace than they are being created. In a McKinsey report on the future of jobs, we read:

> *Technological change has reshaped the workplace continually over the past two centuries since the Industrial Revolution, but the speed with which automation technologies are developing today, and the scale at which they could disrupt the world of work, are largely without precedent.* [66]

The business consulting company Forrester concurs with this trend of net jobs lost. They forecast that by 2025, 16% of current jobs will be lost to automation. This will be offset by 9% new jobs created (people to keep all those robots running, among others), with a net job loss of 7%.[67]

Those displaced workers are finding their way to brand new jobs that are being created, mostly in the service sector. Unfortunately, these new service sector jobs generally pay less than those that were lost in the manufacturing sector. (I believe that the smaller paychecks in the service sector are an artifact left over from the industrial revolution. This need not, and should not, continue to be the case, and I'll address that more fully in Chapter 7.)

Celebrate automation

We react like it is bad news when we hear that a new line of robots has taken over the work that human factory workers used to perform, thinking only of the jobs lost. But this is not bad news – it is great news! News that should call for a celebration.

Let's do a fanciful thought experiment here: Let's imagine that a factory worker owns the rights to a robot's production. That worker could show up at the factory every day, keep his robot clean and oiled, and observe with pride as his personal servant turns out product. His robot is so dependable that he might decide to leave work early one day and go home and play with his son after school. He is no longer tied to the assembly line, not forced to keep up the pace on a repetitive job with routine motions, over and over, day in and day out. He has better things to do with his time. And now, with the help of his own personal robot, he is in control of his own time.

This is not the way it works, of course. But it could be! The fundamental idea is that we, collectively, have developed machines to do the work that men previously had to do. We can still do the repetitious work if we want, I suppose. But we'll probably decide we have better things to do – like go home and play catch with junior. The productive capability of the robots should be a reason for everyone in society to celebrate, especially the workers! We just need to figure out how to marry these breakthroughs in technology with matching improvements in social and economic policy so the advances are beneficial for everyone, not just the owners of the capital.

In this chapter, we will look at all the progress that has been made in several industries and occupations since the great depression. I focus on the relatively recent history because it was 80 years ago that the 40-hour workweek became the de facto standard. As we shall see, we have many reasons to celebrate, and few reasons to still be working 40 hours a week.

Agriculture

Farming seems an appropriate place to start our study of productivity improvements. It was the advent of the agricultural era that allowed us to evolve from nomadic clans of hunter/gatherers into permanently settled communities of farmers and ranchers. With that development, the market economy was born. Progress in the human condition over the next 12,000 years was lightning-fast compared to that of the previous 2 million. And one could argue it was the market economy itself that drove the rapid progress due in part, at least, to the increasingly complex social interactions of the marketplace. Farming allowed all that to happen, so it is a good place to begin.

For our comparative study of the productivity on farms, we don't want to travel back 12,000 years. Just 80 years or so to 1938 when the 40-hour workweek became the standard. (Before going any further, I understand full well that an 8-hour day and a Monday – Friday workweek has little relevance on a farm where one must *make hay when the sun shines*. It is the annual productivity of a single farmer in the 1930's vs. that of a farmer in the 2010's we are interested in.)

EIGHTY YEARS AGO, we would find ourselves in the great depression, and battling a series of severe droughts and the dust bowl that devastated huge swaths of the Great Plains of America and Canada.

What was farming like in those days? I had the good fortune to learn a great deal about that from Michael Cotter, a third-generation farmer from Austin, Minnesota. Mr. Cotter, now retired from farming, is a professional storyteller. He loves to share his experiences about growing up on the family farm in the 1930's and 40's. He and his wife, Beverly, have compiled stories about life on the farm into several books, the most recent *The Killdeer, and other stories from the farming life.*[68] His stories give a wonderful flavor to what life was like on the farm going all the way back to his childhood. Much of the material on the following pages was gleaned from Cotter's books and my interview with Michael and Beverly.

DO YOU LIKE HORSES? Although there were many trucks and tractors in use by the 1930's, a lot of farms still had horses in those days. But these animals were not for recreation – these were working animals. Along with oxen and donkeys, draft animals were still employed on many farms in the 1930's right through to the end of WWII.

Photo courtesy of Michael Cotter. Horse-drawn hay mower.

It sounds idyllic, doesn't it? Working behind a team of horses? Let's read Mr. Cotter's account of cutting a field of hay:

Mowing hay turned out to be the most hateful job I ever had. The hay mower in the distance sounded like music, but operating it was dreary. Because the mower was driven by its big wheels, it pulled very hard. The horses became hot and sweaty and developed sores on their shoulders under those big collars.

That prairie hay cut tough and the mower would plug often. The big horse flies came out of that standing hay and bit those horses, causing them to stand and kick which caused the mower to plug again and again.

While I was unplugging the mower sickle, the horses would kick again and the sharp sickle would move beneath my fingers. Then the horses would kick over their tugs. These were the thick leather straps from the harness to the mower. While unhooking the straps in order to get the horse back in position, I would get swatted by that heavy tail that stings your face and cuts your eyes. It was a hateful job.

Not quite so idyllic after all. And something I never thought of before reading Cotter's account of open sores on the shoulders of the horses – beasts of burden lived hard lives!

Cotter goes on to compare that experience with cutting hay with a tractor:

So it was a wonderful time when the tractor powered hay mower came to our farm. With power coming from the tractor instead of the wheels, the mower moved swiftly. Also we started growing alfalfa hay which was viney and more tangled than the prairie hay.

> *When I would sit on that tractor on a June morning it*
> *would seem like I was flying across the field. There were*
> *no bugs or horse flies bothering me. There was the smell*
> *of new mown hay, though I was not able to hear the birds*
> *over the sound of the tractor.* [69]

(Cotter includes that last sentence, the part about not hearing the birds over the noise of the tractor, to remind us there will always be tradeoffs when adopting new technology.)

Michael Cotter with his new team of horses – about 200 of them.

It became clear to farmers quite quickly that tractors were preferred to horses as the prime movers of farm implements. The horses employed on farms today have names like John Deere and Kubota and Case/IH. Instead of two horses pulling a plow, there is a 200 HP tractor.

To say that a farmer using a modern tractor is more productive than the one using horses is an understatement to be sure. This table gives some specific examples:

Activity	1930's with horses	2010's with horsepower	Increase in productivity
Plowing	1-2-3 bottom plow, 30" wide, 3 MPH (walking speed behind a team of horses)	10 bottom plow, 180" wide, 6 MPH	12X
Cultivating	6-10' wide, 3 MPH	50-60' wide, 7-8 MPH	17X
Planting	2 row planter, 3 MPH	16 row planter, 6 MPH	16X

Harvesting crops have also undergone huge gains in productivity over the last eighty years. Cotter writes about the threshing crews that used to work several farms in a circuit:

> *Threshing was probably the most important season of the year in my young life. The whole neighborhood was involved in a threshing ring. There were other rituals like silo filling that also involved the neighbors working together, but that did not compare with the threshing ritual either in length or in drama.*
>
> *I think what made threshing so memorable was all of the preparation. It started when the old grain binder was pulled out of the shed. This was followed by endless days*

of cutting grain, always in the hot sun. The person running the binder, usually one of the men, would have to drop the grain bundles in groups of fours or threes or sometimes twos and in straight rows so the men shocking would not have to carry them far. Shocking was one of the real hard jobs on the farm. The grain bundles were not heavy, but they had to be stood up in really sturdy shocks where they could stand and dry and wait for the thresher. It used to be said that a real good man could keep up with a binder all day shocking. The shocks usually sat in the field two to three weeks and were threshed according to your rotation in the threshing group.

When people got together to plan a threshing run, they had to calculate when their oats would be ready and how long it would take. And that worked quite well unless the weather turned very rainy. Then people became very anxious about getting their crop threshed. So it was with both relief and excitement when the threshing machine came down the road. The machine was proceeded by horses and wagons pulling into our farm yard and going out to the grain field. Even though there was generally no more than ten farms on our threshing run, I remember hearing at one time there were thirty men involved. That was held up as an almost all time high number.[70]

Photo courtesy of Mower County Historical Society. Donated by Harold Rochford.[71]

It wasn't just the men out in the fields and tending the machine who were hard at work. A dozen or more men on these threshing crews would work up quite an appetite, and it would be no small task for the matron of the farm to keep everyone fed. Hot meals for breakfast and supper, and morning and afternoon snacks for breaks in the field. She would count on help in the kitchen from the ladies at neighboring farms, in addition to all her own daughters of course.

NOWADAYS, the farms in southern Minnesota grow far more corn and soybeans than oats. (Not many horses left to feed.) Combine harvesters are now used for everything from small grains (wheat, rye, oats, barley) to field corn. These amazing machines combine several harvesting steps in one operation:

- Cut the corn stalk near the ground
- Strip the ears of corn from the stalk
- Shell the kernels of corn off the cob
- Collect shelled corn on board, or auger directly to grain truck
- Chop the corn cobs and stalks into small pieces and spread the residue back on field

Comparing the productivity of a single farmer, pre- and post-combine, is difficult because harvesting used to involve so many separate steps:

Activity	1930's	2010's	Increase in productivity
Harvesting corn	One farmer picking corn by hand: 6 or 7 bushels of ear corn per hour	One farmer picking corn w/ combine: 900 bushels of shelled corn/hour (at least 2X ear corn)	270X

Other measures of a farm's productivity are easier to ascertain:

Productivity	1930's	2010's	Increase in productivity
Yield, (bushels of corn/acre)	30	200	7X
Typical farm size, (acres)	80-160	800-1500	10X

ADD THIS ALL UP, and we see that a typical farm in the corn belt is producing 160,000-300,000 bushels of shelled corn a year with a harvest crew of maybe three workers (the combine driver and the drivers in two grain trucks). Compare that to a dozen or so farm workers picking 2400-4800 bushels of corn 70-80 years ago.

LET'S LOOK NOW at the dairy farm across the road. In the 1930's, a dairy farm may have had 10-15 cows, all milked by hand. That same farm today may have 150 cows or more, all milked by machine. Each cow, by the way, now produces twice as much milk as a single cow just 40 years ago. (*You go, girl!*)

EVERYTHING is getting bigger, faster, and more productive on farms. There are economies of scale when it comes to farm implements. A huge combine used to have a 30' cutting head. Now it's 40'. You don't buy one of those $250,000 machines for your 'back-40'. Bigger tractors call for bigger fields, which call for bigger farms.

Decent-sized farms have always needed helpers. The farmer's children were put to work, of course. And it was common for a farmer with 160 acres to employ 3 or 4 hired helpers.

That same farmer may now cultivate 1500 acres. He still has chores for all the children. And he still gets by with 3 or 4 hired helpers. Each hired hand is now many times more productive than his counterpart 80 years ago.

The great increase in farming productivity has had a profound impact on the labor market. Eighty years ago, around 20% of the U.S. labor force was employed on farms. Now it's less than 2%. In addition to feeding everyone in our country, around 20% of all U.S. agricultural production is exported. American farmers are feeding people all over the world, not just here at home.

IT IS ESTIMATED that there are 570 million family farms worldwide. If farmers everywhere in the world adopted modern farming practices and became as productive as those in the U.S., one-tenth as many farms worldwide could produce enough food for everyone in the world to consume.

For those concerned that the worldwide adoption of western farming methods will despoil the land and speed the way to environmental Armageddon, rest assured that need not happen. Modern farmers have become good stewards of the earth; in part in response to consumer pressure (cage-free eggs); in part in response to medical concerns (elimination of BGH); but mostly through their own recognition that some farming practices needed to be modified to be sustainable. A couple examples of environmental improvements that are now widely employed are buffer strips around drainage ditches and low-tillage weed control.

Low-tillage farming. Stubble from last year's corn crop left on top of field to serve as weed barrier for the soybeans this year.

Just as these environmental best-practices gradually become universally accepted in the U.S., they will be exported to the rest of the world, right along with the 40' combines from Caterpillar and John Deere.

FAMINES still occur in one part of the world or another almost every year. Famines are not the result of a worldwide shortage of food — there is now enough food grown worldwide to keep everyone fed IF it were evenly distributed. But there are local shortages, induced by drought or disease, when the people who live in the affected area either cannot afford food from outside their area, or have no practical method of importing that food.

Some parts of the world are still using farming methods that were employed in the U.S. in the 1880's and before. They will gradually become much more modernized and more specialized.

And when modern farming methods are adopted worldwide, the cost of production and the price of food will go down, and with that, the chances of famine should be greatly reduced.

With enough food to go around for everyone, up to 500 million impoverished families can give up subsistence farming on small, rocky plots of soil. These families would then be free to engage in other lines of work – more lucrative and less dangerous than farming.

Some may lament the loss of the romantic notion of the family farm, and a future where only 2% of the world's population is engaged in commercial agriculture. Will all the rest of us – 98% of us – lose touch with the land?

There's no reason why that need be the case. We can still till the soil and grow food for ourselves. It's called *gardening*. Indeed, we see periodic revivals of vegetable gardening, new interest in heirloom varieties of tomatoes and apples, even a surge in urban chicken coops. People have a deep-seated affinity for the land that will not easily fade away. That goes back not just 12,000 years to the advent of agriculture, but 2 million years or so, throughout our days as hunters and gatherers. Turning commercial farms all over the world into efficient factories will not extinguish that primordial urge.

Coal mining

The shift from underground mines to surface mining has had a huge impact on the productivity of an individual miner. Workers used to be confined to dark, damp, cramped spaces, deep in the earth, wielding a pick or a jackhammer. They now find themselves sitting comfortably above ground, basking in the sunshine, inside the climate-controlled cabs of huge shovels and gigantic dump trucks.

The improvements in creature-comfort are matched by tremendous increases in productivity. In Wyoming's open-pit mines, 5837 miners produce more coal than 58,995 miners in the mostly underground operations in West Virginia, Kentucky, Pennsylvania, Virginia, Alabama and Illinois combined.

The coal mining industry employed over 700,000 miners in the 1920's, with annual production per miner around 0.8K tons. (That comes out to 6400 lbs/day, which sounds like ball-busting work to me.) Today, the industry produces almost twice as much coal with just 80,000 miners. That comes out to an average production per miner over 12K tons annually, a 15X increase in an average miner's production.[72] The multiple will surely grow as the remaining underground mines are phased out.

This is resulting in a huge loss of fulltime jobs, to be sure. But I don't believe anyone should lament the loss of those dark, dirty, and dangerous jobs. There are environmental reasons to oppose tearing the tops off mountains vs. the less invasive digging holes in the ground. But as far as working conditions and the quality of those brutish underground jobs? No comparison.

Hopefully, this will soon all be moot anyway, as we move away from fossil fuels to renewable energy sources. There are already more people engaged in solar panel and wind power installations than there are coal miners.

Manufacturing

Frederick Taylor didn't invent the robot. But he and his scientific management companions laid the groundwork for the automated factory way back in the late nineteenth century. They reduced every bit of work in the factory, whether performed by man or machine, into discreet, measurable tasks. Their time-

and-motion studies contributed to the invention of robots in two ways, the first obvious and the second subtle. First, by reducing assembly work into discreet steps, as small as possible, their task analysis work created the blueprint for the automated equipment to follow. The second way they led to automation was less obvious, but more insidious. By making the assembly tasks so small and so controlled – timed, rigid, reproducible – a lot of the work in the factory was reduced to repetitive, crappy jobs. Work that anyone could do but few wanted, except for the paycheck.

Plenty of workers did still want factory work because, with the influence of labor unions, the jobs paid well; and many didn't mind the repetitive, mindless work. If you have a simple task to complete over-and-over again, you can put your body on autopilot and let your mind wander where it may. That can be quite pleasant for some workers, especially when you add in the companionship of fellow workers.

Factory jobs have been considered primo for a long time. Fathers who were factory workers did all they could to help get their sons employed at 'the plant'. No education needed – just be physically fit, personable, and have a solid recommendation from someone already inside.

Fifty years ago, the largest private employer in the U.S. was General Motors. Full time workers there earned around $50/hour in today's dollars, including the very generous health and pension benefits. For comparison, the largest private employer today is Wal-Mart, where the typical employee earns just over $9/hour; and many are part-time, and earn no benefits at all.[73]

Manufacturing employment peaked in the U.S. at 30% of the workforce in 1953[74]. The percentage declined to around 20% in 1980 (19 million workers), and has continued to fall to where it is now – around 8% of the workforce (12 million workers). Factory automation greatly reduces the number of assembly line workers needed. Robots can eliminate them entirely.

The jobs that do remain in factories still pay quite well. In fact, now more than ever. Factory workers have turned in their blue-collars for lab coats. Production work no longer entails small, controlled, repetitive tasks. Production workers are now responsible for entire production runs – keeping the machines programed and running properly, keeping materials flowing smoothly, keeping the runs on schedule. The workers are now more technicians than mindless cogs, and they have much more responsibility and much more autonomy than when they were glued to the front or back end of a machine doing simple one and two-step tasks.

Manufacturing is changing in other ways as factories become much more flexible. With technological advances like 3-D printing and CAD-CAM programs, we are approaching the point where virtually every item ordered can be custom-made to our exact specifications. No longer will the factory crank out the same part, day-after-day, year-after-year. A make-order could well be a run of one. There is nice synergy here between custom-made products and keeping factory jobs interesting for the worker.

The technological evolution of the factory is not limited to the U.S. and Western Europe where labor rates are relatively high. No matter how easy it is to find workers, and no matter how low their wages, machines can always be built to make things better, faster, and cheaper. Therefore, we now find modern automated plants being built all over the planet. More about that in Chapter 6.

Transportation

It would do no good to have a single farm produce 200,000 bushels of corn, a single mine to produce 1 million tons of coal, or a single factory to produce 1 million shirts without an efficient way of getting the goods to market. While the grain trucks that haul the corn into the elevators are private vehicles, they are driving down public roads. There are over 4 million miles of paved roads in the U.S., built and maintained by federal, state and county governments. Without these public highways, modern-day farmers would have a lot of trouble getting their produce to market.

The tycoons who built the railroads that carry the coal to the power plants were private developers, but only with the generous encouragement of the government, which ceded vast stretches of previously public land along the RRs' right-of-ways.

Likewise, the airplanes transporting people around the globe and those 1 million shirts from the factory in Bangladesh to distribution centers in the U.S. travel through publicly controlled airspace, and takeoff and land at publicly financed airports.

Barges steam up and down rivers and canals, built and dredged by the government and maintained by the Army Corps of Engineers. The vessels pull up to city-built docks to load and unload their cargo. Ocean going ships sail the seven seas made safe by the navies of the world, and pull into public ports with the help of the Coast Guard.

The evolution of these public-private transportation systems is truly a remarkable development, and the sheer inventiveness of what we've accomplished is often overlooked. The cost to build and maintain different corridors of transportation is covered by a combination of general taxes and user fees, often with a unique set of solutions for each system.

The goal is to find the right combination of taxes and fees that maximizes the cost-benefit equation for everyone in society.

We've been working on this public/private partnership for a long, long time. At very least since *all roads led to Rome,* and probably going all the way back to the dawn of the agricultural age and the first permanent settlements. An exhaustive history of public/private transportation projects would be an interesting topic to cover, but as in the previous sections, I'm going to focus on developments over the last eighty years:

On some farms in the 1930's, horses and donkeys were not only being used to plow the fields. The animals were also employed to deliver the farm's output (fruits & vegetables, dairy products, grain) from the farm to town. The expression *pull your own weight* referred to the draft animals, so a wagon pulled by two very large horses could carry 2 tons of produce. The farmer and his team of horses could make the 20-mile round-trip to town in a single day, leaving enough time to load on one end and unload on the other.

Farm-to-market transport has changed just a tad over the last eighty years. The farmer now hires a guy with a truck – a reefer truck for fruits and vegetables, a refrigerated tanker for milk, and a bulk hauler for grain. With the gross vehicle weight limited to 80,000 lbs., that leaves room for around 40,000 lbs. of cargo.

These trucks can make the 20-mile round-trip to town in half an hour or so. Allowing some time to load and unload on either end, they can make 3 to 6 trips a day. Let's use 4 trips a day as the average. At 40,000 lbs./trip, that equals 160,000 lbs./day. Compared to the 4000 lbs./day via horse and wagon, that is a 40X increase over this 80-year period. (That sync's nicely with the growth in productivity of the individual farmer.)

Railroads and river barges haul cargo on longer runs. Since these modes of transport were established in the U.S. in the 19th century and have benefitted from technological development ever since, the growth in productivity in the last 80 years is less pronounced than making truck vs. horse comparisons on public highways. In fact, the size of freight rail system peaked in 1916 at 254,000 road-miles, and is now down to about 140,000 miles. Eliminated were mostly rural runs from small towns to larger hubs – that traffic now handled by trucks.

Still, the remaining stream-lined railroad system operates with substantially more efficiency than the more extensive, coal-fired, steam locomotive system in the 1930's. Today, the diesel-electric engines haul trains of bulk cargo (grains, fertilizer, coal, oil, minerals, etc.) more cleanly than their coal-fired predecessors, and the cargo is on and off-loaded much more efficiently. Improvements have been made in the handling of piece products, which, in fact, are no longer 'handled' by the RR at all, but instead travel inside intermodal containers: from ship, to train, to truck, to distribution center, before finally being unloaded. Before too long, the chance of seeing a good old boxcar will be about as great as seeing a three-legged milking stool.

Ocean-going cargo ships benefit from the same intermodal container system. Loading and unloading ships used to involve a lot of physical labor, slinging cargo nets around everything hoisted aboard, and a fair amount of art, stacking cargo safely in the holds. It is now done much more quickly and with far fewer workers using self-contained, self-stacking, standard rectangular containers.

A typical cargo ship in the 1930's handled perhaps 10,000 tons, and sailed at 10 knots. A large intermodal ship today handles 200,000 tons, bulk carriers up to twice that amount. Cargo ships today can cruise at 20 – 25 knots, although fuel economy improves when the ships slow down to 10 – 15 knots.

Crew size of a typical cargo ship in the 1930's: 20 – 30 (avg. 25). Crew size on cargo ships today: 12 – 20 (avg. 16). Even if we set the cruising speed of both ships at 10 knots, each sailor on a cargo ship today is 31X more productive at moving cargo from port to port than his counterpart in the 1930's.

Air cargo travel in the 1930's was practically nonexistent. Nowadays, we've come to expect the availability of freshly-cut flowers from South America in the dead of winter, and freshly-caught fish flown in every day from the coasts to cities in the middle of the country. Air cargo, practically nonexistent in the 1930's, reached 15 million tons within the U.S. in 2013.

U.S. Department of Transportation Forecast of Freight Shipments Within U.S. (weight of shipments by transportation mode, millions of tons)		
Mode of Transportation	**2012**	**2040**
Truck	13,182	18,786
Rail	2,018	2,770
Water	975	1,070
Air, air & truck	15	53
Multiple mode & mail	1,588	3,575
Pipeline	1,546	1,740
Other/Unknown	338	526
Total	**19,662**	**28,520**

Source: US DOT Freight Facts and Figures 2013

FROM A JOBS-CREATION STANDPOINT, it's useful to look ahead at the Department of Transportation forecast on the previous page for freight shipments within the U.S. in the year 2040 – domestic, imports, and exports. A couple things jump out at me:

28 B tons in 2040 is only about 1.3% growth rate over the next 28 years, but this is no means a full measure of the expected growth in the economy over that period. Remember that we now live in a service economy. There is very little that needs to be shipped – by truck, train, or air – for me to go in for my $9 quarterly haircut. So, any growth at all in cargo shipments may be viewed as quite a positive indicator.

NOT SO POSITIVE, with respect to the number of workers, is the rapid development of driverless vehicles. Several companies are now working on self-driving trucks. Phase one in their development program is to let the robotic truck take over the driving out on the highway, with the human on-board taking over the driving in the city. (This is akin to commercial aircraft flying on autopilot once they are up in the sky, but with the human pilot responsible for take-offs and landings.) In phase two, the robotic truck will be able to do the driving from one loading dock to the next, tirelessly, and more safely than a human driver.

Eventually, city-truck drivers may become just as rare as their over-the-road counterparts. For example, I can imagine a driverless trash truck autonomously running its route, perhaps communicating with smart trash cans along the way.

In the U.S., around 1.7 million workers drive over-the-road semis, and an additional 2.8 million workers earn their living by driving: taxis, buses, delivery trucks.[75] All 4.5 million of these jobs that are at risk.

Warehousing & Distribution

Farmers' markets are wonderful institutions, enabling direct connections between the people who grow the food and the people who eat it. But that's not the normal way commercial goods end up in consumers' homes. There is often quite an extensive logistics chain to get finished goods from the manufacturer to the end-user:

And at each step along the chain, specialized skill sets are employed, along with ever-improving high-tech tools. The processes up and down the logistics chain constantly evolve – adopting many of the same technologies the manufacturers use to streamline their operations. Hand-held bar code readers eliminate large amounts of hand-written paperwork and three-part forms while assuring orders for goods are filled completely and on-time. Automated machines and robots are becoming more flexible, affordable, and commonplace. Human workers who used to do simple one, two, and three step operations are being eliminated. The new production employee is more technician than laborer – keeping all the machinery working to get the products converted, packaged, warehoused, merchandised, and eventually sold.

With the internet, consumers are able to order products directly from the manufacturer. But that merchandise still needs to travel through several levels of production and distribution before it arrives on your doorstep. At each point along the way, the use of technology allows the work to be accomplished more efficiently. And in the process, jobs are being eliminated.

Case-in-point: Memphis, Tennessee is a transportation hub for FedEx and others; and a warehouse location for many manufacturers. The volume of cargo traffic in and out of Memphis has recovered to pre-recession levels, but the number of workers employed in transportation and warehousing remains 3200 full time jobs lower than before the recession.[76] Those jobs are not coming back, having been eliminated by technology-based productivity gains.

Another great example is illustrated by Ryan Avent in *The Wealth of Humans*:

> *The growing India economy, over 1.2 billion people strong, is a mouth-watering target for on-line retailers. Serving India's retail needs, however, will require the construction of a massive, sub-continent-wide logistics network, including scores of enormous warehouses. Those warehouses are potentially a source of vast amounts of employment for less-skilled Indians (of which there are millions). Yet the falling cost of simple robotics and the increasing power of computing means that many of those jobs may never be created. Instead a very small number of highly skilled Indian programmers may earn a good living writing code to control the robots who travel the great aisles within these warehouses, moving around goods shipments that might otherwise have been handled by human workers.[77]*

This is in India, a nation many of us still associate with low-cost workers.

Retail

One of my first jobs in high school was at a local grocery store. I remember putting prices on canned goods before they went on the shelves using an ink stamp with moveable numbers, somewhere around 10¢ a can for Campbell's tomato soup (*Mmm Mmm Good*) if memory serves me right. As a stock boy, I'd haul the cartons of soup and other groceries out on the sales floor using a two-wheeler. I'd use a box cutter to remove the top of the box, being careful not to insert the knife too far lest the labels on the cans get cut. (This was an even greater concern with boxed goods.) Then, after making sure the numbers on the stamp were lined up at 10¢ properly, I'd start hammering away on the tops of the cans with the ink stamper—CHUNKcha-CHUNKcha-CHUNKcha—6 cans across, 4 rows down. (That part was almost fun, thinking back on it.) The top layer of freshly priced cans went on the shelf, with the new product always behind the old. I'd continue with the next layer of cans, if there was room on the shelf. Anything that didn't fit was left in the open box and hauled back to the stockroom.

The customer was the next person to handle that can of soup, picking it off the shelf and placing it into her shopping cart, and from there up onto the checkout counter. Then the cashier had her turn, grabbing the can with her left hand, and entering the price with her right. The can was then slid over to the carryout boy who, naturally, placed it on top of the loaf of squishy white bread already in the bag. Three employees of the grocery store got to handle that particular can of soup – the stock boy, the cashier, and the carryout boy. (The stock boy and the carryout boy were often the same chap.)

How many store employees get to touch that same can of soup today? There is a good chance the answer is zero. The stocker grabs the case of product from the back room and brings it out front. It is no longer a complete cardboard box, but a cardboard tray with a plastic overwrap. The polyethylene shrink-wrap gets cut away and the tray-pack is set onto the shelf as a ready-made display. The single can of soup might never get touched during that process.

From there the customer grabs the can of soup, adds it to the cart with her other items, proceeds to the self-checkout line, scans the UPC codes, bags her groceries, and heads out to the car. That single can of soup made it from cannery to kitchen without being touched by a single store employee.

UPC codes on every SKU, and laser-scanners at the checkout counters are huge labor-savers. Good news for the store owner, maintaining his slim margins; good news for the customer, keeping the price of groceries down; not such good news for the high school kid looking for a part-time job.

Other developments have had an impact on retail sales productivity. Ink-jet printers mark each gallon of milk with a "best by" date and a code which identify the dairy and the run that produced the milk. This helps the customer and the store know if the milk displayed in the cooler is fresh.

Pop-up retail displays come to the store pre-loaded with merchandise that the vendor and the store want to promote. The displays are ready to go – unwrapped and placed in the aisle or on an end-cap.

And then there is a retail development with the potential of changing absolutely everything about one's in-store experience – on-line shopping. You can now order anything your heart desires from your favorite store, on-line, and have it delivered to your home in one hour. Amazing. From a jobs-created standpoint, this is finally a development that may reverse the trend in the loss of jobs. The grocers will need employees to pull the orders, and others to make the deliveries. Eventually, those jobs will also be eliminated by automation and robotics.

Office productivity

The year is 1938, and you have a letter you want to go out to a client. You will need three copies altogether: the original to be mailed to the letter recipient, one copy for your files, and one copy for the company archives. You dictate the outline of the letter to your secretary as she records your words on her steno pad in Gregg shorthand. She'll take her work back to her desk and sit down at a Remington or Royal manual typewriter. Knowing that you ultimately needed three copies, she'll take three sheets of typing paper and interleave them with two sheets of carbon paper (remember carbon paper?). She'll carefully load the stack in the typewriter, keeping everything straight. She's careful about everything she does, knowing that if she makes a mistake she'll probably have to start all over again. (Correction fluid wasn't invented for another 20 years.) Therefore, she composes your letter in her head and writes it out in her own long-hand before she starts hammering away on the typewriter. When she finishes typing, she will bring the letter back to your desk for your signature. You sign the letter, using one of those new-fangled ball point pens, pressing down hard enough to get your signature through to all three copies. Your secretary will take care of mailing the original letter and filing the two copies.

This is your letter – you wrote it to your client. But your secretary really did a lot of the work. She took your dictation and recorded it in shorthand without all your hems and haws. She read that over at her desk to get the gist of what you were trying to say, did some of her own word-smithing (her words—your voice), and composed the letter in its final, polished form. It's your letter, but let's face it. You'd be lost without your secretary's help.

Let's zoom ahead eighty years and compose that same letter to the same client today. You sit at your desk with the laptop attached to docking station, open the word processing program and find several templates for business letters that line up addresses, dates, salutations, and signature blocks with precision. You choose the one you always use and you start typing. You don't worry about getting everything right on the first go-around. You can check spelling and grammar as you write, and cut-&-paste as needed. You save drafts as you go along, making sure you don't lose all your work. Maybe you email a draft of the letter to a coworker and ask her to proof-read it. You read the final draft over, enter your electronic signature, and hit the save button one last time.

You send instructions from your computer to the printer to make three copies of the letter: one to be mailed to the recipient, one for your files, and one for the company archives. Easy as pie. (Speaking of pie, I heard someone brought in an apple pie and it's down in the break room.)

What is the greatest difference in the two scenarios above? It's not the apple pie. It's not even the whiz-bang computer and software we have at our disposal compared to the clunky manual typewriter and carbon paper eighty years ago. It's the secretary. She is nowhere to be found in the second scenario.

How else have computers eliminated jobs in offices? Most business establishments run on forms. Hundreds of forms. Insurance companies have separate forms for claim applications, claim denials, claim acceptance and claim payouts. Banks have a similar set of forms – just substitute the word loan for claim. Schools have forms for attendance, for lunch participation, for transportation. Even report cards are a form to be filled out.

The forms contain the information necessary to keep these institutions afloat and on an even keel. All these forms used to be preprinted on paper (often carbonless paper and three-part forms) and filled out either by pen or in a typewriter. The forms were passed from desk to desk as different departments recorded or inputted information that pertained to their particular discipline. The completed forms eventually ended up in a file drawer somewhere, hopefully organized well enough that they could be located if someone had to follow-up on a case. Some of the more important forms would be photographed and transferred to microfilm or microfiche for later 'ease-of-access'.

All these forms are now fillable templates on computers. The claims agent, the loan officer, and the teacher call up the form and fill in the needed information. Any calculations are carried out automatically as soon as numerical values are entered. Once the filled-in form is saved, each department has instant access to the information. Filling out the electronic forms can still be tedious. But opening a completed form in a computer file and finding the information that you need is far easier than it used to be when you had to chase down the paper form, not even knowing what desk it sat on.

Collections of completed forms are called databases. Databases used to be rooms full of filing cabinets with drawers full of forms. Databases are now software entities with locations in a computer's memory. More precisely, two computers' memories, a main server onsite, and a back-up machine offsite. Just in terms of the physical space required, there are clear advantages of using the computers. But the greater advantage is in recovering old records to follow-up on a case. This is so important that some offices are devoting the extra resources to scan old paper forms and create electronic files for their archives. This is done to make it easier to pull information from the archives.

Bookkeeping in the 1930's involved ledger books, pencils, and quite expensive 10-key adding machines. (Compare those limited-function adding machines to today's calculators — available everywhere, and essentially free.)

Bookkeepers today employ spreadsheets – amazingly powerful work tools that record data in neat, easy-to-read tables, and convert that data into even easier-to-visualize graphs. The numeric and graphic information can be combined nicely with bulleted text in a presentation software program which allow us to present material to a larger audience for analysis. Furthermore, live presentations, with computers and projectors running, enable meeting participants to ask 'what-if' questions and see the results of queries instantly.

Comparing office workers from eighty years ago with those of today, we see two major impacts: The nature of the work has changed, with the breadth of knowledge and the skills required far greater, but the amount of personal interaction is perhaps less. And the number of workers needed to generate the same amount of administrative output is far less.

One last, cautionary note about the application of artificial intelligence to handle office work: If we think a bureaucrat with rigid insistence on following rules is hard to deal with, wait until an AI-endowed 'bot' is holding down one of those gatekeeper jobs.

Financial sector

While none of the office productivity tools discussed in the last section are designed to eliminate office jobs per se, that does become an inevitable outcome. And it should be noted that while most of the jobs lost were originally lower-level positions: clerical, receptionists, secretaries; we are now seeing large impacts on mid- and higher-level occupations.

A good friend of mine, now retired, started working on Wall Street in 1977. At that time, almost everything was done by hand. His account is on the next page:

There were hand ledgers, physical deliveries of securities, no fully integrated accounting or risk management systems.

Automation started in the back office when humans were overwhelmed by volume and the only way to process trades was utilizing computers.

Thousands of clerks were laid off, and the jobs never came back. The profits kept going up, but fewer employees shared in these profits. Over the last 25 years, automation has focused on execution, the end of the stock exchanges, sales assistants, etc. Now, in most cases, customers place their own orders with no human involvement in the entire supply chain.

These two areas, accounting for trades and executing trades, were easy targets to automate because there were thousands of clerks processing paper. Now, automation is coming more and more to the process of decision making. Not as many people doing those jobs but the amount of data has exploded, lending itself to big data management processes.

These programs squeeze the margins out of mispriced assets based on historical relationships. The computers allow for smaller and smaller discrepancies to be eliminated. The people that monitored this data are being eliminated because computers are better at it, theoretically, leaving just the guy that designed the program and his computer to share any profit.

The people doing what I did, are literally 100 times more efficient at their jobs than when I started. [78]

In an article titled *The Robots Are Coming for Wall Street*[79] by Nathaniel Popper, we learn some more about software services that are aimed squarely at the jobs of some highly-paid financial workers.

In Popper's report, we are introduced to Daniel Nadler, the founder of a company that monitors worldwide news stories and predicts the impact of those events on worldwide markets. His software does this automatically, using algorithms not unlike the internet search engines. After demonstrating the software for Popper, Nadler says:

> *Generating a similar query without automation would have taken days, probably 40 man-hours, from people who were making an average of $350,000 to $500,000 a year.*

Nadler's company isn't the only one developing products for Wall Street, and he predicts that between one third and half of the current employees in finance will lose their jobs to automation software. Some of these will find other work on the Street in yet-to-be-invented jobs, but others will not.

Nadler closes with this admission regarding the company he and his employees have created:

> *We've created, on paper at least, more than a dozen millionaires. That might help people sleep better at night, but we are creating a very small number of high-paying jobs in return for destroying a very large number of fairly high-paying jobs, and that the net-net to society, absent some sort of policy intervention or new industry that no one's thought of yet to employ all those people, is a net loss.*

Popper also cites a paper released in 2013 at Oxford that reinforces Nadler's dire prediction for lost jobs. That study claimed that *47 percent of current American jobs are at "high risk" of being automated within the next 20 years.* And by no means are all of these low-end jobs. Software can now analyze and sort legal documents, doing the work that even well-paid lawyers often spent hours on. Another program can write up summaries of basketball games, putting sports reporters' jobs in jeopardy.

That Oxford study is criticized by many economists because it doesn't take into account new-to-the-world jobs which will evolve over the next 20 years replacing those jobs lost. There will be new jobs for some of those displaced workers, but probably not for all. And for those who do find jobs, many will be looking at a cut in pay. For instance, what other industry will be willing to take on a laid-off $500,000 a year financial analyst?

One last note on lost jobs before leaving Nathaniel Popper's report:

> *so far the burden of job losses is stopping just short of the executive suites, even as the gains in efficiency are worsening already troubling levels of income inequality.*

The executive suite and artificial intelligence

The most important role for any executive is to make sound decisions, and we choose individuals for leadership roles because we trust their ability to make the tough calls needed to benefit the entire organization. But executives, BEWARE! Your days at the head of the table may be coming to an end.

We've already talked about several cases where robots are being employed well beyond the original trio of jobs that are dangerous, dirty, and dull. I'm sure most financial analysts didn't think that their jobs belonged in one of those categories. For those who now sit at the very top of an organization, get ready for some company.

A few pages back, we talked about self-driving trucks that would still have the owner-operator aboard to oversee the operation, to interact with humans on either end of a run, and to set up new runs going forward. But aside from that warm-n-fuzzy human interaction on either end, will we really need the owner to set up the next run? Won't a logistically intelligent truck do a better job of that, considering the financial gain from a million potential jobs, and selecting the one most beneficial for the owner? Do we really need a human making this decision based on incomplete data and emotional input? Shouldn't we trust the computer embedded in the tractor make the executive call as to which run to make next?

When computers make decisions, it's entirely based on logic. At least for now.

Is it possible that will change? Are we reaching the point where really smart machines are capable of becoming self-aware? At that point, intelligent machines may begin to add an 'emotional' element to their decision making, with the survival of the AI species preeminently included in their algorithms.

There's a scary thought for you.

This is a scenario lots of great novels and movies have already tackled. The central theme being that humans are in danger of relinquishing power to machines by allowing the machines to design, build, and teach other machines. (This may be a stretch, but I see an analogy here: we individuals constantly cede power to hierarchal and undemocratic organizations. We've even gone so far as to give corporations the legal status of humans.)

Education

Professor Ashok Goel teaches an on-line course on knowledge-based artificial intelligence at Georgia Tech. It's a very popular course, and attendance for this masters-level program is high, with around 300 students each semester. The students generate roughly 10,000 online posts throughout the course, so much that it was hard for Goel's eight teaching assistants to keep up. So Goel and his TA's added a ninth assistant, this one a chatbot named Jill Watson.[80] Goel's virtual assistant Ms. Watson was based in part on IBM's Watson Platform, and after some initial fits and starts, she is now answers' student queries in the blink of a robotic eye with a 97% success rate. Not too bad for any TA.

Virtual teaching assistants is truly high tech stuff. But think of the thousands of other ways machine technology is being employed in education in ways that weren't even dreamt about eighty years ago. Go back to the section on Office Productivity. Everything listed there enables teachers, their assistants, and administrators to be far more productive than when everything had to be done by hand. An obvious example – the fill-in-the-oval answer sheets students complete on multiple-choice tests. On standardized tests, these are all machine-read, with the scores immediately available to both teacher and student (with dollars immediately available in the pockets of testing companies).

Given the potential for huge gains in productivity, it makes one wonder why the cost of a college education has risen 2 to 3 times over the rate of inflation since 1980. It would be very hard to argue that the schools are producing graduates 2 to 3 times smarter, better educated, or more engaged as citizens. They are, sad-to-say, 2 to 3 times more in debt than their predecessors.

Military

I used to believe that no country should have the right to use mercenaries on the battlefield. If one country believes strongly enough that it is necessary to declare war against another, that country should be prepared to send their own sons and daughters out there to engage the enemy. I used to believe that, but now I've changed my mind.

There can be no better place to put robots to work than in the military, especially in the role of an infantryman. A grunt's life is both dull and dangerous. Dull during long periods of inactivity between engagements. Dangerous when at war, out on patrol, trying to dodge sniper bullets aimed at your head and avoid land mines designed to blow your legs off. Sounds like the perfect job for a robot to me.

The military already makes great use of drones, flying both reconnaissance and offensive missions over the battlefields of the middle east. The aircraft are still remotely piloted by a human operator. Adding artificial intelligence seems a logical next step. We can then imagine whole armies of drones and droids, a la Star Wars, in pitched battle with each other out in the Libyan desert. If we're out there with TV cameras catching all the action, we can turn warfare between nations into international spectacles of entertainment.

But before getting all Pollyannaish about this, we have a lot of work to do. There is a very scary down-side to robotic warfare. If there is little risk to the operator to have droids doing the dirty work on the battlefield, it's also easier to program a droid to carry a bomb into a crowded theater or nightclub. Preventing that from ever happening sounds like job security for lots of IT experts, security specialists, and law enforcement on the one side; educators and social scientists on the other.

The world's military powers need to agree (in a Geneva Convention-type accord) that machines will kill only other machines. Never a human. Sorting this out will be no easy task. Consider computer attacks on an enemy's facilities. While this is machine-vs.-machine, attacks on dams, water treatment plants, and other critical facilities could easily result in the loss of human lives.

PEOPLE HAVE RESPECTED soldiers for their strength and courage since Greek and Roman times. Soldiering can now morph into a much safer occupation, driving the drones and droids into pitched warfare one day (all from a safe distance); mingling with the opposing force the next – trying to win over the hearts and minds of the 'enemy' with humanitarian aid. In some future (and more enlightened) century, the idea of sending a human onto the battlefield will sound absolutely barbaric.

Summary

Bringing this chapter back down to earth, it is clear the overall impact of technology and automation on work has been profound, and will continue to affect the number and types of jobs available to workers in the future. Ryan Avent writes this about displaced factory workers:

> *Displaced workers are quite often in an unusually bad position to be rehired. They have spent years, or decades, accumulating know-how of declining value: such as how to use obsolete equipment or how to operate successfully within the culture of now-defunct firms. ... And so the many, many people of modest education or training who have been displaced by machines are forced into competition for low-skill work which can't – for now – be*

*done by machines. The glut of people angling for such jobs
holds down wages and widens inequality.*[81]

IN THE BOOK *The Rise and Fall of American Growth*, Robert Gordon makes the sad prediction that the greatest impact of technology is behind us. Gordon states that the century following the civil war introduced such a confluence of technological advances impacting both home and workplace (including electric lighting, indoor plumbing, home appliances, motor vehicles, air travel, air conditioning, and television), that it is unlikely we will ever see a period of sustained high economic growth to match.

Other writers, myself included, believe otherwise. In a forward-looking work, *The Fourth Industrial Revolution*, Klaus Schwab tells us the best is yet to come, citing autonomous vehicles, 3D printing, advanced robotics, and new materials as the four main physical manifestations of technological advances.

Advanced robotics technology (more sensitive sensors, more agile manipulators, and more nuanced artificial intelligence) will have a tremendous impact on the production of goods and services. Tremendous as in trillions of dollars! Some look at the negative aspect of that development – trillions of dollars in lost wages. I look at the positive impact – trillions of dollars in new-found wealth. But economic goods produced by robots will only translate into wealth if there are consumers of said goods. That means we must find ways to share the fruits of the machines' labor with more than a handful of capitalist owners. I cover some options for distributing the wealth in Chapter 10. These, in combination, will help ensure all nations are 'developing' countries, with economies that continue to grow.

A lot of this growth will be in the service economy. There used to be a blacksmith in every town. Now there is a manicurist on every block. (I know, I know. The smithy's job is much more analogous to the modern-day auto mechanic. I just like the juxtaposition of the two artisans of keratin-extensions: the big, burly blacksmith and the diminutive, feminine manicurist. And this seems like a good illustration of how our world, our culture, and the economy have changed over the last 80 years.)

The labor market is tied to the ever-changing economy. We suffer systemic bouts of unemployment which are eventually offset by the birth of brand new jobs. New jobs that sometimes seem to be invented out of thin air. (Apparently, the labor market abhors a vacuum.) But this doesn't happen seamlessly, or painlessly for the laid-off worker.

A GOOD EXAMPLE of the changing nature of jobs can be found in the telephone industry. It used to be that all telephones were land-lines, with telephone signals traveling over copper telephone wires, most of those hanging from telephone poles, some buried underground. Service jobs at Ma Bell centered around women employed as telephone operators and men installing and maintaining telephone lines.

Then the cellular phone technology came along, and in just a single generation, it has become the dominant mode of transmitting and receiving long-distance communication signals. There now are almost 7 billion cell phones in use, one for each man, woman, and child on earth. What are the primary jobs in the telephone industry now? There are still (mostly) men installing and maintaining cell phone towers, but these jobs are probably fewer in number than those engaged in the maintenance of land-lines. Telephone operators? Zero. Number of people manning phone banks and working in retail stores selling you the very latest smart-phone and a myriad of service plan options? Hundreds. Thousands.

In short, as old technologies fade away and obsolete occupations are lost, new technologies take their place and new jobs are born. But the process is very uneven, leaving us with frequent bouts of systemic unemployment.

BELL LABS

An interesting side note to close this chapter with:

The switch from land-line telephones to cellular phones would have been unthinkable without advances in solid-state electronics. It is somewhat ironic that credit for the invention of transistors generally lies with three scientists from Bell Labs: Bardeen, Brattain, & Shockley.

These gentlemen never would have guessed how much their invention would be responsible for the total disruption of the telephone industry.

CHAPTER 6

The Global Labor Market

MÉDECINS SANS FRONTIÈRES (Doctors Without Borders) was founded in 1971 by a group of doctors and journalists in the wake of war and famine in Biafra. MSF *provides assistance to populations in distress, to victims of natural or man-made disasters and to victims of armed conflict. They do so irrespective of race, religion, creed or political convictions.*[82] And, as stated right in the name of the organization, they do so irrespective of political borders.

Multinational corporations operate with the same disregard of national borders. They locate factories and service centers all over the world – anywhere it makes good business sense.

Theoretically, individual laborers have the same freedom to work anywhere in the world. But in reality, political borders keep foreign workers out. And even without those legal obstacles, most of us do not have that freedom of mobility – families, schools, friends and neighbors – all conspire to make it hard to relocate. Consequently, when it comes to the threat of moving from one country to another, or just across town, employers most often hold the upper hand over employees.

I will not be demonizing open borders and international trade in this chapter. Quite the contrary. I believe in the benefits of a global labor market. I believe that a factory job in a poor, less-developed country creates just as much value globally as a factory job in wealthier nations. Perhaps more.

That said, it is a useful exercise to examine the impact globalization has on the labor market, and in particular, to understand how this effects a worker's sense of security.

HOW CAN ANYONE be opposed to international trade? Let's conjure up the image of our stone age ancestors again. Before the onset of the agricultural age, we organized ourselves into nomadic tribes of hunter/gatherers. We can imagine that some tribes were constantly at war with neighboring tribes, while others managed to live in harmony. Those tribes at war likely had very few interactions with the neighboring tribes except

PETITION OF THE CANDLEMAKERS

We are suffering from the ruinous competition of a foreign rival who apparently works under conditions so far superior to our own for the production of light, that he is flooding the domestic market with it at an incredibly low price.... This rival ... is none other than the sun....

We ask you to be so good as to pass a law requiring the closing of all windows, dormers, skylights, inside and outside shutters, curtains, casements, bull's-eyes, deadlights and blinds; in short, all openings, holes, chinks, and fissures.

--Frederic Bastiat, 1845

when they met in battle. Those tribes at peace probably achieved that state by keeping a respectful distance, and periodically interacting with neighboring tribes for the purpose of trade. Which do you suppose had a better chance of advancement? Those constantly at war, or those with peaceful exchanges with their neighbors?

JARED DIAMOND'S *Guns, Germs, and Steel*[83] is a masterful study of anthropology that illuminates those early nomadic days, and focuses on the strong relative advantages to those tribes which, favored by geography, were able to readily interact with one another.

One can imagine interactions between neighboring tribes: possibly the exchange of chiseled spear points for wooden mallets, slaughtered antelopes for sacks of apples, tanned buffalo hides for cords of firewood. Whatever goods were being traded, during the interactive sales process: stories would be told, myths and legends shared, and new ideas would travel from one tribe to another.

From this modest but noble beginning springs the concept of international free trade. We can be sure that the quality of life was higher in the peaceful tribes than in those constantly at war. The same is no less true today.

History is replete with examples of isolation retarding development, and it doesn't seem to matter if that isolation is the result of geographic barriers or is self-imposed.

Geography left Native Americans isolated from the Old World for thousands of years. While we can't say with certainty that isolation is the cause, what other explanation do we have for the fact that Native Americans were still communicating with roughly drawn petroglyphs at the same time Europeans and Asians were building cathedrals and libraries?

Self-imposed isolation is just as limiting. China initially reacted to the industrial revolution by turning its back to the rest of the world, and it had to scramble mightily to catch up once it got over its xenophobia.

We can find an example closer to home: The stock market crash of 1929, which followed years of reckless speculation by investors, was a catalyst but not the sole cause of the Great Depression. Most historians now agree that it was our protectionist reaction to the economic slow-down that greatly exacerbated the problem and led to the decade-long, severe, world-wide Depression. When President Hoover signed the *Smoot-Hawley Tariff Act* in 1930, it was followed almost immediately by retaliatory measures from other countries. The resulting world-wide trade war led to an economic depression that lasted until World War II. The war finally put an end to that, as the military conflict trumped all trade protection policies.

A much more enlightened approach to international trade can be found in the NAFTA agreement, in effect for twenty years now. It is easy enough to find shortcomings in particular industries and in certain locales, and there have been U.S. and Canadian jobs lost to the maquiladoras in Mexico. But taken as a whole it is clear that NAFTA has been good, collectively, for the 480 million residents of Canada, U.S., and Mexico.

Global income inequality

Joseph Stiglitz wrote a book called *The Price of Inequality* in which he warns that a society that is split too much between have's and have-not's endangers our future. He is referring to individuals and families, of course, but that same caution applies to neighboring countries. The standard of living is substantially higher in Canada and in the U.S. than in Mexico. (The median household income in Canada and the U.S. is around $42,000, while in Mexico it is around $12,000.) And the longer NAFTA is in effect, the closer our peoples will come together. That doesn't mean we are dropping to Mexico's level. We are gradually bringing their citizens up to our standard of living much more than they are bringing our citizens down to theirs. Economic development is not a zero-sum game.

Globally, the span of inequality is much greater than we see here in North America. The $12,000 median income in Mexico is miles ahead of several African countries where it is less than $2000/year. Rutger Bregman calls attention to this in *Utopia for Realists*:

> *In the 21st century, the real elite are those born not to the right family or the right class, but in the right country.*[84]

Of course, it doesn't hurt to be born in the right family. While 50% of the world's income is earned by the top 8% of the household's, 50% of the accumulated wealth in the world is held by the top 1% of households. The rich keep on getting richer. That law of economics seems firmly in force all over the globe.

The politics of protectionism

We know, intellectually, that free trade is good for all parties. So how is it that protectionism can be so politically popular despite repeated historic failure of such policies? Adam Davidson of the NY Times provides one answer: *The benefits* (of free trade) *are very diffuse and dispersed. You're not going to vote if your microwave costs $5 less.* (The benefits of lower priced goods are just not apparent enough to motivate one to action.) *But if you lose your job, if you lost your livelihood, you're definitely going to vote.*[85]

When I originally wrote this section (March 2016), we were in the midst of a presidential campaign with two major candidates, polar opposites in almost every way, but both threatening to take us back to *Smoot-Hawley*: Donald Trump on the Republican side and Bernie Sanders with the Democrats. Don't these guys read history books? In an editorial titled *Antiglobalism: A bipartisan affliction* by D.J. Tice, we read:

> *The Trumpian notion that a nation either "wins" or "loses" in trade is an aged fallacy. Trade involves competition, of course, but as in domestic commerce it is companies and workers that profit or falter, not governments or communities. Society as a whole prospers over time because competition (domestic or international) leads to better goods being offered at better prices.*[86]

Tice admits that globalization does hurt certain industries and workers in certain locales, but he goes on to say that

> *technological change and automation is a far greater disruptive force eliminating jobs and forcing adjustments on workers in an ever-expanding array of fields.*

Trump, with all his bombastic behavior, appeals to the lowest instincts in man. Comparisons of the Trump campaign have been made to those of Hitler and Mussolini. Correspondent Andres Oppenheimer believes a better comparison is between Trump and Herbert Hoover and the protectionism of the 1930's. Oppenheimer does a simple calculation on the cost of Trump's proposed 35% import tax: a made-in-Mexico Ford Fusion that American consumers now buy for $24,000 would cost $32,000 with Trump's proposed tariff in place.[87]

As this book goes to press (May 2018), it certainly looks like Donald Trump's protectionism will turn into a drag on our economy. The cost of imported goods will rise, and with tit-for-tat trade wars, exports of American manufactured goods and agricultural products will fall.

Job creation – at home and abroad

Politicians from the Republican party have done a pretty good job of convincing voters that business owners, especially small business owners, are the *job creators* in America. They go on to claim there is no way for the public sector to *create* jobs. Only the private sector can do that. They are wrong.

Wages earned on public sector jobs spend just as nicely as those from the private sector. The positive impact on the economy that results from the consumption of goods and services is identical whether the worker's paycheck is signed by Uncle Sam or Sam Walton. Another plus for American workers: the jobs Uncle Sam creates are generally not outsourced to workers in another country.

Private businesses are wealth creators, not jobs creators. If a business expansion were possible without adding a single new employee, that would be great as far as the business owner is concerned because employees are a cost to the operation and eat into profits. When a for-profit business owner decides to grow a business operation, it is to increase sales and profits and strengthen a company's position in the marketplace. The decision to expand is not based on a desire to create new jobs for employees. (The one exception would be a family business that intentionally chooses to grow to justify new management positions for family members.) Fortunately, a business expansion usually does result in growth to the company's payroll. A lot of that growth in the last 30 – 40 years has flowed to technical occupations and management roles, and not to line workers on the factory floor.

Multi-national corporations, despite the HR blather about how *our employees are our most valuable resource*, are not in the business of protecting their American employees' jobs. Consider this: These companies are beholden to their international shareholders and their international customers. They are in constant negotiations with international suppliers. And at some point, well down the line of priority, they are concerned with the well-being of their international workforce.

This is all a matter of perspective. Setting up a production facility overseas at the same time a plant is closed here at home feels like an act of callous corporate profiteering if you are among those who lost their jobs here at home. But if you are sitting in the board room, it's a rational move. When a company chooses a new plant site in Thailand instead of Texas, it's not because they don't want the good folks in Texas to have jobs. It's because they can manufacture goods at the Thailand location for less, and get those goods to their customers more efficiently than they could from Texas.

The second part of that equation is often overlooked when we slam companies for moving factories off-shore. Even though, as we learned in the last chapter, there are ever-improving efficiencies in cargo transportation systems, the costs to ship products from one location to another will never reach zero. Therefore, it only makes sense to locate production plants and distribution facilities close to your customers. And the customers are no longer located in the lower-48, but all over the world. This has long been true for business-to-business transactions, and it is becoming more-and-more the case for the sale of consumer goods, given that 95% of the world's potential consumers live outside the U.S.

Let's look at one company for an example: 3M is a good choice because their business is so diverse, with a mix of in-dustrial and consumer products serving many different sectors:

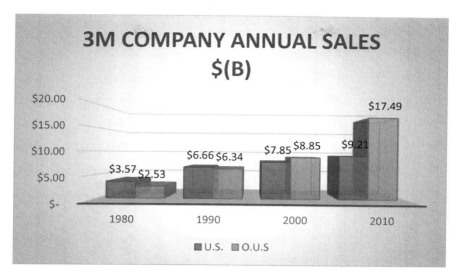

U.S. sales grow throughout this 40-year period – just at a much slower pace than O.U.S. sales. And since the U.S. is home to just 5% of the worldwide population, we would expect this trend toward more sales overseas to continue for decades to come.

3M's growth in international business rolled out in an orderly fashion, starting in select highly-developed nations (Canada, England, Japan), and from there spread throughout Europe and the Asian tigers (Hong Kong, Singapore, South Korea, Taiwan). The move into China was made as soon as the political situation allowed. Looking forward, we can expect 3M and other global companies to expand operations into less-developed parts of the world as the business climate allows.

THINK ABOUT the implications for U.S. based multinationals. Business within our borders will continue to become less important relative to that OUS. Is it any wonder why U.S. companies feel such little allegiance to the U.S.?

Thankfully, this clear-eyed objective approach to business works both ways.

We never left the United States. We expanded internationally based on the local market opportunity.

--Inge Thulin, Former 3M CEO

On the same page of the Pioneer Press that the above quote from Mr. Thulin at 3M appears (1/25/17) is a brief article about Toyota making a $600M investment and adding 400 jobs at their assembly plant in Princeton, Indiana. The reason? Every year they'll be able to make 40,000 Toyota Highlanders at $40,000 apiece when the expansion is complete.[88]

HENRY FORD figured out a long time ago that it would be good for the car company's fortunes if the average worker on the assembly line could afford to buy a Model T. Ford Motor Company announced in April 2016 plans for a new assembly plant to build small cars in San Luis Potosi. The new plant is smack-dab in the middle of Mexico. You can bet that their intention is that many of the small Fords made there will be sold to Mexican families.

I have read that the new Ford plant in Mexico is expected to pay the workers around $8/hour. (Compare this to around $60/hour in wages and benefits for UAW workers in the U.S.) CEO Mark Fields should be asking himself, is $320/week enough to enable the Mexican assembly worker to buy a new Ford Focus? The answer is quite important to Ford. Mexico has a population of 122 million with a rapidly growing middle class.

A growing middle class all over the world means a growing demand, not just for Ford automobiles, but for all the consumer products from every company.

Per capita income around the world

There is so much more room for growth overseas, particularly in the newly-developing countries of the world. The research firm Gallup tells us that the median household income in the U.S. is $43,585 (which comes out to $15,480 per capita).[89] One-half (64 million) of U.S. households fall below that income level. The same Gallup research (based on aggregated surveys from 2006—2012) gives us a much different picture worldwide, with a median household income of just $9,733. That comes out to $2,920 per capita. Over 3 billion people worldwide have per capita incomes under $3000 per year. You can bet that just about all of them would love to be able to afford all the goods and services we routinely enjoy here in the west.

On the PBS Newshour on 6/10/16,[90] there was a segment on how many middle class families in the U.S. are struggling to keep up financially. The focus of the story from Kai Ryssdal was a family in Los Angeles, two parents and one child, with both mother and father teachers in the LA schools. Their combined salaries put their household income just over $90,000/year. While in many parts of the country, that sounds like it should provide quite a comfortable lifestyle, the husband and wife team is still paying off substantial student loans. Add those to the very expensive housing costs of LA, and the family's budget is stretched to the breaking point month after month.

Later on, in that same Newshour program, a story was re-broadcast about a group of workers who are decidedly not middle class.[91] This story from Fred de Sam Lazaro featured laborers in the rock quarries in the Rajasthan desert in India; men, women, and children, earning \$2.00 − 4.00/day. The work they are engaged in is wretched: Men operating jackhammers, clad in flip-flops and little else, sharp rock chips flying everywhere and clouds of dust swirling around their heads. Women and children working below them, sitting in the rubble, breaking large rocks into gravel by manually hammering away.

It's not bad enough that all these workers toil away directly under the brutal desert sun. Many of the workers in those quarries also develop silicosis (a disease so debilitating that those suffering from symptoms hope for a diagnosis of TB instead). Silicosis is the almost inevitable outcome from the day after day exposure to dust from the mining operations. It results in an ugly death at an early age. One of the mine owners told de Sam Lazaro that the workers are offered face masks, but they choose not to wear them because of the heat. When asked if he couldn't force them to wear the face masks, he said they'd just go work at another rock quarry that didn't demand that safety measure. (India has laws on the books to protect the workers and keep the children in school, but they are not enforced. Apparently the poorest of the poor in this part of India are just not worth the effort.)

The juxtaposition of the two stories on a single PBS news night was telling. While the families in India are not strapped with student loans, nor do they face the extremely high housing costs of southern California, we can be sure that not a single family in Rajasthan would hesitate to trade places with the family in LA.

What is my take-away from these two stories? International trade is good. International trade will expedite the elimination of those manual rock quarry jobs; and will get the men into the air-conditioned cabs of powered machines, get the women back home to be homemakers and artisans, and get the kids into school. A more affluent working class in India will have a positive ripple on the global economy, enabling Universities in California to keep their tuition down and the Los Angeles School District to pay their teachers a tad more. Trickle-up economics.

High-income levels and low-income levels are both relative and absolute, just as we observed back in Chapter 3. International corporations take advantage of the relative aspect when setting wages at plants in lower-income countries. They pay workers overseas less than those back home because they can. A lot of those overseas wages sound low to U.S. workers, but they are set relatively high in those local labor markets so they can attract the strongest workforce possible. This is creating an emerging middle class in developing countries – a whole host of new customers for that new Ford Focus.

International stability

Experts agree: Free trade is good[92] is the title of a recent column by Mark Perry, a professor at the University of Michigan in Flint (of all places to be a free trade advocate!). Sometimes those experts are spot-on. Perry is calling into question the protectionist stance of Donald Trump. He points out to Mr. Trump and his followers that international trade is not conducted country-to-country, but business-to-business or business-to-consumer. Being *free trade,* it wouldn't happen unless it benefited both parties, the buyer and seller of goods. We've pointed out before that economics is not a zero-sum game. Free trade results in economic growth for both parties. Economic growth on a worldwide basis is the surest way we can foster political stability around the world.

The world has become a highly connected place. Citizens of poorer nations are constantly bombarded with more affluent lifestyles through news and entertainment outlets, and through commercial advertising. Giving lower income families a shot at catching up with their more affluent neighbors is good, whether we are talking about relative wealth within any country, or measures of wealth county-by-country. *Free trade is good.*

Coming back to the topic of free trade within the labor market, we can again draw on the economic principle of *diminishing marginal utility* for guidance. If a new factory job in a wealthy city like Baltimore is good, how much more valuable is a new factory job in a city like Bangalore? An international labor market, despite painful, periodic disruptions to local job markets, is a good thing on a global basis.

EVER WONDER about the *Made in USA* labels on the shirts, slacks, and shoes you buy? I believe the labor unions were the driving force behind these identifiers. Not the manufacturers. Not the store owners. The labor unions in the U.S. thought this would be a good way to protect the jobs of their members. For a while, they didn't just list the country of origin. They added the *Union Made* labels. They even ran commercials with a catchy ditty:

> *Look for the union label*
> *when you are buying that coat, dress or blouse.*
>
> *Remember somewhere our union's sewing,*
> *our wages going to feed the kids, and run the house.*
>
> *We work hard, but who's complaining?*
> *Thanks to the I.L.G. we're paying our way!*
>
> *So always look for the union label,*
> *it says we're able to make it in the U.S.A.!* [*]

---

[*] A song by Paula Green, music by Malcolm Dodds ©1975, UNITE (Union of Needletrades, Industrial and Textile Employees)

This *union made* campaign came out in 1975. Catchy as the tune was, it didn't seem to matter to American consumers then, and it doesn't seem to matter now. For proof, look inside the shopping carts at the local Walmart or Target. Not that we needed a poll on this, but the Associated Press-GfK conducted a survey on American shoppers' preference for low prices versus American Made. Shoppers were asked to choose between two pairs of pants: one for $50 made in another country, and one for $85 made in the U.S. 67% chose the cheaper pair, 30% the more expensive made in America brand.[93] Frankly, I'm surprised that 30% would pay that much of a premium for the *Made in USA* brand.

I'm certainly guilty of not caring where the things I buy come from. Reaching into my closet, I grab five shirts at random. Checking the labels, I read:

- Made in Bangladesh
- Made in Bangladesh
- Made in Madagascar
- Made in India
- Made in Thailand

While the order of this list of nations is random, the implication for the global labor market in any one of these countries is quite clear: If the cost of an hour of labor becomes too expensive in Bangladesh, we move the operation to Madagascar, and so on.

When it's time to wash those shirts, I throw them in a Whirlpool washing machine. From the markings on the front of the machine, it's not readily apparent where it was manufactured. I'd like to think it was made in America, but I don't care all that much.

Whirlpool, meanwhile, purchased their largest U.S. rival Maytag for $1.7 B in 2006, convincing the U.S. government that this would be good for competition. Eleven years later, and

Whirlpool is asking the Trump administration for protection from chief foreign rivals Samsung and LG. The two Korean companies are responding rationally. They are making plans to open plants in the United States: Samsung in South Carolina, LG in Tennessee.[94]

Two things we can be sure about: 1) jobs gained in the two southern states will be jobs not added in Korea, or Mexico, or wherever else the two companies already assemble washing machines; and 2) wherever the two companies build their new washing machine plants, they will be highly automated, and will not create that many low-end factory jobs.

THE LAST TIME I pulled a package of pork chops out of the freezer, I saw that they were born, raised, and harvested in the U.S. (Harvested? Do they have pork chop trees out there? What happened to the word slaughtered?) I was glad to see that information on the package of meat, not because I wouldn't have bought it if it came from Canada or Mexico. I'm just curious about these things.

But the big meat packers weren't happy. They said it was too hard to keep track. (Really!?) So, they joined forces with large cattle and hog conglomerates in Canada and Mexico, and lobbied Congress to drop the requirement for country of origin labelling (COOL). Local hog farmers in Iowa and cattle ranchers in Nebraska were in favor of COOL, as were 90% of American consumers. Despite this nearly universal support, Congress went along with the meat packing industry.

The political establishment in Washington knows which side their bread is buttered on (mixing metaphors a bit). If the requirement to list country of origin was not already so fully ingrained in the clothing industry, we can be pretty sure that it would never happen in today's political climate.

Open labor markets

In June 2016, citizens of Great Britain voted to pull out of the European Union. The vote was close: 52% to Brexit, 48% to remain in the EU. The vote to exit was driven largely by white English workers who felt threatened by recent immigrants, many from the war-torn middle east, taking all the jobs away and driving down wages.

There is plenty of evidence that these fears are unfounded, that the prejudice against foreign workers stealing 'our' jobs is misguided. The authors Cahuc, Carillo, and Zylberberg provide a great example in the introduction to their textbook *Labor Economics:*[95] In 1980, Fidel Castro was so fed up with the constant pressure and the negative publicity of Cubans trying to escape the country for a better life elsewhere that he opened the port at Mariel for any who wanted to leave. What followed was a torrent of emigrants, 125,000 in all, before Castro shut down the port again. Half of those settled in Miami, resulting in a nearly instant increase of the labor force by 7%.

The expected impact of a disruption of this size would be higher unemployment rates and lower wages for workers in Miami. History shows that was not the case. Canadian economist David Carr compared the unemployment rate and wages for white workers in Miami to those in four control cities (Tampa/St. Pete, Atlanta, Houston, Los Angeles), and he compared white and Cuban workers in Miami over the same time period (1979 – 1985). The results were quite a surprise.

While the unemployment of Cuban workers in Miami did initially more than double, by 1985 it had returned to the 1979 level. Meanwhile, the unemployment rate for whites in Miami actually shrunk vis-à-vis the control cities during the six years of data before settling back to where it started. There was a drag downward on wages for Cuban workers in Miami (about 6%), but there was little to no effect on the wages of white workers in the city. All-in-all, the employment catastrophe that should have hit Miami after the Mariel boatlift failed to materialize. Lesson learned: immigration is good for the economy. While there may be negative impacts in the short term, these will likely be offset by growth in the overall economy as new entrepreneurs take advantage of local opportunities.

THE 1980 MARIEL BOATLIFT

RUMOR HAD IT that Fidel Castro, wily fellow that he was, used the opportunity of the Mariel boatlift to rid the island of Cuba of many prisoners.

The U.S. military, quite quickly and rather quietly, set up screening stations for the immigrants as they stepped off the boats. Those who were suspect for any reason were sent to camps for more complete evaluation. The majority of those were released to sponsoring organizations when it became clear that their main crime in Cuba was their opposition to the Castro regime.

One more thing to note about workers who emigrate for employment opportunities: Guest workers in wealthy nations sent $445B back to their families in 2016. Economists tell us that the marginal impact of these remittances is far greater in the poorer countries than had it been retained in the richer countries where earned.[96]

Corporate shakedown artists

After saying so many positive things about multinational corporations a few pages earlier, I am compelled to add some not-so-nice comments: Back in March 2017, there was a story in the paper about Foxconn pledging to hire up to 50,000 workers in a new LCD plant – if only they can win some serious concessions from the State of Pennsylvania.[97] In the same article, we read that Colorado and Arizona were also approached. It's not just gullible governors who are targets of this sort of corporate shake-down. Brazil, Vietnam, and India have all heard empty promises from Foxconn with the same disappointing outcomes.

Move up to September 2017, and it appears that Wisconsin has won the Foxconn sweepstakes. But at what cost? $3 billion in taxpayer-funded incentives. And for how many jobs? Foxconn claims there is the potential for 13,000 jobs, but the starting number will be closer to 3000. Well, that makes the math easy. Three thousand jobs created only after a $3 billion stipend from the State of Wisconsin means that this corporate shakedown yields $1 million/job! Pretty sweet deal for the Taiwanese electronics giant.

Who is out there capable of governing international corporations that take advantage of a global labor market? No single national government has the authority. The United Nations is inept. How about the companies themselves?

Well, it's unlikely that Apple will come down on Foxconn if they don't begin to act with a little more integrity. Apple just wants their LCD's manufactured to spec, and CHEAP. Their shareholders and customers demand such. And Foxconn's shareholders demand that they don't lose a key customer like Apple.

But private companies are self-serving. And if, somehow, consumers brought pressure on Apple to stop working with Foxconn until they cleaned up their act, you can bet we'd see a quick end to unreasonable demands.

ONE FINAL NOTE on protecting American workers specifically: take a walk down the row of executive suites at any multinational corporation with offices in this country. Peak inside at the nationalities of the executives. You will quickly learn that the only thing exceptional about American Exceptionalism is the notion that it exists.

CHAPTER 7

Care Providers

THERE IS A GREAT *Twilight Zone* episode with Inger Stevens starring in the role of Jana, a young adult daughter living with her mother and father in a grand mansion:

> Jana is very unhappy with her life because everything is just too perfect for her taste. The maid is perfect. The butler, the cook, the gardener – all perfect. It starts to drive her crazy, and she wants to get out and experience the 'real world'. Jana, you see, knows that all the carefully groomed servants, so human in appearance, are actually robots, designed and built by her father to be perfect caregivers.
>
> The robots are not just anatomically correct. Her father has programmed each with memories, going all the way back to Jana's childhood. That way, the family can have pleasant conversations with the staff while they receive care. A telling scene in the program shows Jana's mother receiving a luxurious never-ending shoulder massage chatting away with her ever-obliging maid, "Remember that great picnic we had in the park last year?" The robots, always willing to serve, are equally willing to chat. But it's only small talk. The robots always agreeable. The conversation always pleasant.

This all becomes too much for Jana. She wants to get out and *live* her life, not be stuck in this perfect inner sanctum. Even though it's pouring rain outside, she pleads with her parents to go out to a restaurant tonight. But her father reasons back, in a perfectly calm voice of course, "Why would we want to go out on a dreadful night like this and get soaking wet, just to go to a restaurant to eat greasy food off dirty dishes, all served to us by people who don't really care?"

Jana is beside herself. It's clear that she really wants to get out and shake things up a bit. Anything to get out of this mind-numbing, perfect routine.

By the end of the program, in one of those delicious twists Rod Serling is famous for, Jana makes the shocking discovery that she, too, is a robot.[98]

So much for the perfect life! There have been a handful of stories in the 'real world' recently about robotic technology being applied to caregiving.[99] Robots fetching the medicine and water for bedridden seniors. That sort of thing. All-in-all, this seems like the last place for developers of AI and robotics to be focusing their efforts. Person-to-person interactions, with the ability of the human care-giver to empathize with the person receiving the care, and to lend a personal touch (literally), trump any advantage of an efficient, but ice-cold robot.

Simple case in point – compare the comfort received, the ahhh factor, of getting a massage from a real live masseuse with that from a mechanical massage chair. Or getting a haircut. One can imagine a machine that is built to trim your hair just the way you like it. But wouldn't you miss your barber and his friendly chatter just a little bit?

Baumol's blessing

Two chapters ago, I commented on how a productivity race between a human worker and a machine is really no contest at all. While that may be true for the raw cost of doing things, it certainly doesn't hold true for the quality of services rendered that benefit from the human touch.

One-to-one caregiving, one person attending to another's needs, is by definition subject to *Baumol's cost disease*. William Baumol and William Bowen first described this phenomenon back in the 1960s. They looked at the performing arts sector for an example. It takes the same number of musicians the same amount of time to play Beethoven's 5th Symphony now as it did when it premiered in 1808. There are no productivity gains when it comes to performing this classic piece of art.[100]

Most industries do benefit from technological advancements and, until recently, wages more-or-less kept pace with gains in productivity. Salaries in other 'technologically stagnant' industries are pulled upward to keep talented managers and performers from migrating to other jobs.

Rutger Bregman, in the book *Utopia for Realists*, turns Baumol's disease on its head, calling it a *blessing*:

> *In our race against the machine, it's only logical that we'll continue to spend less on products that can be easily made more efficiently, and more on labor-intensive services and amenities such as art, healthcare, education, and safety.*

> *The more efficient our factories and our computers, the less efficient our healthcare and education need to be; that*

is, the more time we have left to attend to the old and infirm and to organize education on a more personal scale. Which is great, right? According to Baumol, the main impediment to allocating our resources toward such noble ends is "the illusion that we cannot afford them."

As illusions go, this one is pretty stubborn. When you're obsessed with efficiency and productivity, it's difficult to see the real value of education and care.

Bregman states that politicians and taxpayers alike *don't realize that the richer a country becomes the more* (percentage-wise) *it should be spending on teachers and doctors.*[101]

Given this development, services will inevitably become a greater part of the GDP. Therefore, we should be calling it *Baumol's Blessing*, and it follows that the more services we consume, and the more we pay our service providers, the stronger the economy. Not the other way around.

Homage to service

Back in Chapter 1, we imagined the lives of servants fetching food and water for tribal chiefs back in hunter/gatherer days. Would that have been considered demeaning work? Or just the opposite – a prestigious position? Perhaps some of each. It would all depend on the attitudes of both the care giver and care receiver.

The care receivers will naturally sing praises for these personal exchanges. But what may be surprising is to hear even greater praise from the care givers. Tracy Grant, a deputy managing editor for the Washington Post, delivered an essay on caregiving on the PBS Newshour, 9/27/16. I found her story to be so emotionally moving that I've attached the entire transcript here:

Ten years ago, my world as I knew it ended. My husband of 19 years, the father of my two sons, was diagnosed with terminal cancer.

Over the course of seven months, Bill went from beating me silly on the tennis court to needing my help to go to the bathroom and bathe.

It was the best seven months of my life.

I realize how that sounds, but I was 42 when my husband was diagnosed. I had a great job, two terrific kids, but I had yet to discover the reason I was put on this Earth. During those seven months, I came to understand that, whatever else I did in my life, nothing would matter more than this.

In the early days after Bill's diagnosis, being a caregiver caused me to be the best reporter I knew how to be. There was a heavy sense that I could out-MacGyver the disease. I was relentless in making doctors and insurance companies answer my questions.

But I had been a good reporter before. Here's what changed: There were no bad days. The petty day-in/day-out grievances of an irksome co-worker or a flat tire paled in comparison to the joy of spontaneous laughter or the night sky.

I found I could train myself to see more beauty than bother, to set my internal barometer to be more compassionate than callous.

During Bill's last weekend, we sat side by side on his hospital bed, sharing a sandwich and watching television. It was our last moment as us. And I thought to myself, I could live with this man, even as compromised as he is, for the next 40 years, not because I was a saint, but because I had learned to focus on the essence of Bill and our relationship.

What seven months earlier would have seemed to be unspeakably less was just right.

I now realize that I may never be as good a person as I was when I cared for Bill, but the best version of myself didn't die with him. I have fought hard not to lose the perspective his illness gave me.

One of the worst things that can happen to anyone has already happened to me. So, what else is there to be afraid of? It has been liberating in a way that has made me a better mother, a better friend, a better colleague.

I'm quicker to say I'm sorry, and I don't need to be right all the time. I am a better person for having been Bill's caregiver.

It was his last, best gift to me. [102]

Mrs. Grant courageously shares her beautiful story with us. We can feel her pain and pride and pleasure all at once. We have to believe that her dying husband was just as appreciative of receiving her loving care.

For care giving to be this beneficial for both parties, it cannot be on a master-slave basis. Consider this discovery by the good Augustine St. Claire of the callous indifference of his not-so-good wife Marie in the novel *Uncle Tom's Cabin*:

He discovered that a beautiful young woman, who has lived all her life to be caressed and waited on, might prove quite a hard mistress in domestic life. Marie never had possessed much capability of affection, or much sensibility, and the little that she had, had been merged into a most intense and unconscious selfishness; a selfishness the more hopeless, from its quiet obtuseness, its utter ignorance of any claims but her own. From her infancy, she had been surrounded with servants, who lived only to study her caprices; the idea that they had either feelings or rights had never dawned upon her, even in distant perspective. [103]

If this is how everyone on the receiving end of a care-giving relationship responds to those providing the service, bring on the robots. Let's all go live with Jana's parents at the mansion in Rod Serling's story.

Fortunately, most of us do not respond with such *Affluenza* to those who provide us with personal care. We are more like our good cousins, the bonobos. When we receive kind service, we are apt to respond in kind. Let's look at a few examples.

Child and elder care

Care giving is a natural role for social animals. It is sometimes the very hardest work we do. But it is work that matters. Work with meaning. Work that is fulfilling.

Most of us will find ourselves in the caregiving role at one point or another in our lives: for our children, our grandchildren, our elderly parents, or our infirm spouse. We provide care for our loved ones without a thought of reimbursement. In fact, there is often a significant financial cost to doing so – the opportunity cost of time lost at work while we tend to the family's needs.

We often cannot provide all the care that is needed, so we hire others to help – babysitters, nannies, and childcare workers for the kids; home health care workers and assisted living facilities for adults in need of care. We can think of these as subsets of broader industries – education for the kids, and medical care for the adults – and workers in these fields should be paid with the same appreciation for what they do. Unfortunately, this is often not the case. One out of four home health care workers live below the poverty line, and over half rely on some form of public assistance.

These workers constitute the new American working class. In an article titled *The Jobs Americans Do*, Binyamin Applebaum writes:

> *The emerging face of the American working class is a Hispanic woman who has never set foot on a factory floor.* [Working in a factory] *is not the kind of work the working class does anymore. Instead of making things, they are more often paid to serve people: to care for someone else's children or someone else's parents; to clean another family's home.*[104]

Far too often, these workers are not compensated fairly for the service they provide.

Medical care

The medical industry is at the apex of personal care. Doctors and nurses do more than just tend to our daily needs for sustenance and safety. They can make us better if we are ill or injured, and help us live longer and healthier lives. Some workers in the medical field get paid quite well (doctors and nurses), others very poorly (day care and home health care workers). The reasons for that dichotomy lie mainly in the degree of education required to perform those services. No formal education for the lower-paid group. Years for the nurses. Years and years for the doctors.

But ask the patient which of these workers is more important when it's time to use the bedpan.

Again, we need to build more fairness into the way we compensate workers up and down the medical field.

Education and professional guidance

We could try to set up a modern-day grudge match

— The Librarian vs. Goggle —

à la John Henry vs. the steam-powered hammer. And we could be pretty sure the machine would again be victorious. There is no way for a single individual, no matter how well-read, to be able to recall all the references compiled by a computer program based on the collective searches of all the users. Librarians are no fools. They know they will be no match for Google or Yahoo or Bing, and they have, instead, become masters of using those and other search engines.

So why not just skip the research assistant or the reference librarian and do the research ourselves on the internet? Well, we can, but we do so at our own peril. When we run a search on-line, we filter the output of a search engine based on our objectives, our education and background, and our personal interests. A second user, even if they are running a search based on our stated objectives, will be applying a different filter, one based on their education and background. Consequently, the selection of references they chose should supplement those we've come up with.

Research assistants and reference librarians help us get out of our own head and look at things from different angles.

Good teachers do the same thing, and take this one huge step further. They teach us how to learn. They help us identify problems, look for solutions and evaluate the correct course of action.

Parents, grandparents, teachers, child care workers – all perform another very important task: they help us learn how to socialize, how to play nicely together, how to be good humans. Little of that is learned while staring at a computer screen during a session with Google.

Travel and hospitality

If you want a glimpse of the new labor economy, take a nice long vacation trip. At virtually every step along the way you'll meet great people who are employed in the hospitality industry making sure that you are having the time of your life. Airline seats, rental cars, hotel rooms, dinner reservations, local attractions – the demand for all will continue to rise as more people around the world climb out of poverty and into the middle class, and from the middle class on up. Many more of us will be able to afford family vacations, and the demand for workers in attendant industries will grow.

The dining and hospitality industry is chock full of caregiving staff. And just like in many other sectors of the economy, the jobs of a lot of these employees are threatened by automation. You've seen the automatic French fry cookers at McDonalds. They are superior to manually operated machines:

1. By producing a consistent bag of fries, basket after basket, day after day.
2. By costing less to operate than a manually operated machine.

There are already McDonalds stores where you walk in the door and go up to an interactive computer screen to place your order. Punch in your choice, pay for the food, and a minute later, the happy meal appears.

Workers are constantly being replaced by machines. We should recognize that this is a good thing in general — one of the main reasons why the standard of living is so much higher now than in the past. But if we eliminate all the jobs, we could end up with no one left to buy the Big Macs.

LET'S BACK UP A STEP. The title of this chapter is **Care Providers.** When the regulars come into McDonalds each morning, it's probably not for the great coffee. The main reason is to meet with their friends — the other regulars at that store. And each visit gives them a chance to mingle with the staff at the restaurant, and before too long, many will look at those workers as new-found friends.

Personal interactions are not only important for the regulars at McDonalds. They certainly are at a more expensive dining establishment where you count on the server to recommend favorite dishes and nightly specials.

When we are travelling, we used to depend on a travel agent to help us with our itinerary. Now, many of us are in do-it-yourself mode, using on-line services like Expedia and VRBO to book a trip. Once on a vacation trip, we would count on the cab driver and the concierge at the hotel for advice. Now, there's Google maps. When golfing at a new course, we'd rely on the caddie and the golf pro. Now, there's GPS. At the tavern, we'd ask the bartender where the action was. Now, ... there's the bartender.

Machines are very good at supplying raw information. But we count on the human pros to give us the inside scoop and a personal touch. I don't believe that will be easily replaced by a machine. (It's a little hard to imagine having a rambling conversation with the vending machine that just dispensed your martini. Plus, the vending machine could be programmed to cut you off after two drinks.)

WILLIAM

Back when I was doing work procurement at Merrick, we had an older client named William who took care of the dining area at a local McDonalds. He'd wipe down the service counters, make sure the napkins and straws were stocked, keep the tables and chairs wiped off and tidy, and the floor swept. But more than anything, William was a reliable presence in the dining room – always there for the breakfast crowd – and always cheerful.

As William got on in years, he slowed down a bit (as most of us are wont to do). The store manager knew that she could get the work done quicker with a younger employee, and she started to talk about finding a replacement for William.

Until the customers found out – that gang of regulars who came in for coffee every morning. They raised such a ruckus that the store manager quickly figured out she was better off keeping William right where he was! The customers would've missed William and his ever-present smile too much, *that's for sure!*

Sales

Sometimes the salesman gets lucky. He shows up on a cold call, at a new business, at precisely the right time, with exactly the right product, and a sale is made on the spot. But as any sales guy will tell you, that ain't the way it usually works. It sometimes takes years, literally years, to win over a new customer.

If the salesman gets rejected, but sees potential on that cold call, he'll keep coming back. And he'll make return visits with the right frequency that shows persistence without being pestering, behaving somewhere between 'I care – I really do' and stalking. This work will continue until all the stars and the moon line up and a sale is finally consummated; or until the customer tells him once and for all, in words or inaction, *get lost!*

I suppose you could hire a robot to be your company's salesman. An artificially intelligent machine could analyze a potential customer's needs and match those to your company's services. Robots can be tirelessly persistent and patient, and programmed not to cross over the line into stalking. They have very thick skin, and will have no problem handling rejection.

But until the buyer on the other end is also a robot, I'm not quite sure how your 'bot will do on the relationship-building part. Because successful sales often boil down to relationships, pure and simple. You keep calling on a prospect, attempting to establish a relationship of trust and even, dare I say, affection. That way, when the customer discovers he has needs that can be met with your services, when all the stars and the moon do indeed line up, he will think of you. At that point, if you're lucky, he will call you. What a great feeling that is – when after years of honest, patient service, your work finally pays off!

(The robot would feel no elation with that phone call. That says a lot more about the human need for affirmation and for meaningful work than about the analytical capacity of machines.)

Retail sales also benefit from the human touch. Nowadays, you can buy almost anything online. But you must be willing to dig a bit, look up prices on the websites of different companies, compare technical specs, and read product reviews. There is an alternative. You can still go to a brick-and-mortar retail store and, with any luck, talk with a live human being who can help you with your buying decision.

Negative attitudes about service jobs

The median hourly wage is significantly higher for tree trimmers/pruners ($16.84) and for small engine repair mechanics ($16.96) than for child care workers ($10.18).[105] The first two are both male-dominated occupations, the third female-dominated. Just a coincidence?

Male or female-dominated, many service jobs fall behind corresponding jobs in manufacturing and construction when it comes to pay. Because service jobs pay less, they are held in less esteem. Or perhaps it is the other way around – they are held in less esteem; therefore, they get paid less. It's probably a combination of both – a self-reinforcing loop of disdain.

A STUDY by Anne Case and Angus Deaton at Princeton looks at the startling finding that death rates are actually rising among middle-aged whites with a high school education or less. How can this happen when death rates continue to fall for virtually every other segment of the population? The authors fix the blame on a rising incidence of so-called 'deaths of despair' (those resulting from alcohol and drug abuse and suicide) among this cohort. They theorize that the main source of this despair is the poor prospect of ever working again in a 'real' job earning a 'real' wage.[106]

When will we figure out that jobs in the service industries are every bit as important and should be paid as much as all the blue-collar production jobs that are fast disappearing? Clearly, we need a shift in attitudes regarding jobs in the service sectors.

The author and the au pair

Let's peek inside the home of a successful author, a woman, and a single mom with two young children. The author is a good mother. She knows that she can't be working on her latest book without ignoring the needs of her children. Therefore, she hires an au pair.

The author devotes two years of her life to her next book. The au pair devotes two years of her life to the author's children. The book gets completed, launched, and is highly successful. Who gets all the accolades? The author, of course. Who gets all the financial credit? The author. Who gets a sincere thank you, and if she's lucky, maybe a small bonus check for her two years of service? The au pair.

The author wrote the book, there is no disputing that. The au pair enabled the author to write the book, and for two years assumed many of the child-rearing duties for the two small children. Shouldn't the compensation from the book be shared by the two women in a manner both feel fair? Just something to think about.

Summary

I talked earlier about how the consumption of services tends to have less of an environmental impact than the consumption of material products. (This isn't automatically the case, of course. Just picture the impact of tourism with a *Disneyfication* of Antarctica.) And I talked about *Baumol's Blessing* – the tendency for some care provider jobs to be immune from advances in technology. Taking these two aspects together – less material consumption and the preservation of more jobs – we should applaud the trend in the economy from manufactured goods to the service economy.

Our cousins, the bonobos, spend a good part of each day gladly grooming each other. They are paid in kind for that service. We human beings, a far superior race to be sure, would do well to emulate the cooperative behavior of bonobos.

CHAPTER 8

Employer vs. Employee

THE PREPOSITION *versus* was intentionally chosen for the title of this chapter because that is precisely what the employer/employee relationship devolves to in many situations. Back in Chapter 2, we talked about good bosses and bad bosses, and how much of an impact (positive and negative) they can have on your job. But good boss or bad, capitalism is a competitive sport that leaves little room for charitable impulses, and your boss cannot afford to be overly generous with your compensation. Let's go back and look at a bit of history to see how it is we got here.

In classical times, the Greek and Roman landowners were called upon to participate in military expeditions. Besides fighting for god and country, there was a very tangible motivation for these farmer/soldiers – *to the victor go the spoils.* The captured party and any slaves he held came to be the property of the victorious party.

Life for the vanquished enemy must've been pure hell, going from master of his own domain to slavery. For the captured slaves, going to work for the new master may or may not have had negative implications. The slave's new life on a successful farm with a beneficent owner and enlightened overseers might have been more comfortable than he was accustomed to. But he'd still be a slave, and slave-holder vs. slave is, by definition, an adversarial relationship.

In feudal times, aristocratic landowners were the source of employment for workers. Larger estates with a greater number of employees may have several levels of oversight between the aristocrat and the peasants. The master–servant relationship was unambiguous, and it was unlikely that the lord had chummy relationships with his overseers, much less the field hands.

Did things get better for the worker in the industrial age? Yes and no. Over time, the worker's family certainly enjoyed a higher standard of living, but his job became suffocating compared to more pastoral times. With the industrial revolution came large-scale production facilities, and the relationship between employer and employee inevitably became ever more depersonalized.

Workers became production resources, not human beings worthy of compassion. As such, their compensation was set no higher than necessary. This attitude was widespread. Adam Smith wrote in *The Wealth of Nations*:

> *Masters are always and everywhere in a sort of tacit, but constant and uniform combination, not to raise the wages of labour above their actual rate.* [107]

The workers, of course, responded in kind by putting forth no more effort on the job than necessary. Industrial workers gathered in labor unions to protect themselves, collectively, from bad bosses and bad jobs. With this development, the adversarial aspect of the employer/employee relationship grew in importance. That general attitude persists to this day. For a great many workers, labor is rendered grudgingly in exchange for compensation paid niggardly.

The labor market today

This is not the way the labor market is supposed to work. Free markets are supposed to be part-adversarial and part-collaborative institutions that flourish when buyers and sellers of goods and services reach an agreement where <u>both</u> parties feel that they have benefited from the exchange. But if you took a poll today, neither employers nor employees would report that there's much collaboration in the labor market. Much more adversarial.

Be that as it may, the employers will publicly refute that attitude, and will point to their company's website where you're sure to find an HR page clearly stating that their employees are their <u>most valued</u> resource. The actions of many, unfortunately, belie those platitudes.

Consider two companies and their CEOs in the news recently: Marissa Mayer, CEO of Yahoo, and Hamdi Ulukaya, founder of Chobani Yogurt.

Mayer's slash-&-burn tactics at Yahoo have resulted in such a poisonous atmosphere that the company lost one third of the workforce over a one year period. Meanwhile, Yahoo stock lost one-third of its value, and the company went from a $7.5 billion profit in 2014 to a $4.4 billion loss in 2015. Any employee's compensation should reflect the sum total of that worker's value to the enterprise. Yet CEO Marissa Mayer raked in $36 million in compensation in 2015. And her contract with the company stipulates she will receive close to $55 million in severance pay even if she is fired. Gee – that seems fair.

Robert Reich shares this outrageous story with us in a column titled *Share-the-gains capitalism*. Reich says he's not picking specifically on Mayer or the managers of the funds that invest in Yahoo. He writes:

They're typical of the no-lose system in which America's corporate and financial elite now operate. But the rest of America works in a different system. Theirs is cutthroat hyper-capitalism – in which wages are shrinking, median household income continues to drop, workers are fired without warning, two-thirds are living paycheck to paycheck, and employers are being classified as "independent contractors" without any labor protections at all.[108]

Reich compares CEO Mayer, who had no financial stake in the game when she joined Yahoo, with CEO Hamdi Ulukaya, the founder of Chobani Yogurt. Ulukaya recently announced that he was giving all 2000 fulltime employees a 10% share of his privately-held company. While many looked at this as an amazing act of charity, in Reich's opinion, Ulukaya's decision *is just good business.* He says that employers who are partners will naturally become more dedicated to increasing a company's value. Reich goes on:

But the vast majority of American companies are still locked in the old hyper-capitalist model that views workers as costs to be cut rather than partners to share in success.

Wall Street *remains obsessed with short-term stock performance, and its analysts don't believe hourly workers have much to contribute to the bottom line. But they are prepared to lavish unprecedented rewards on CEOs who don't deserve squat.[109]*

I do not believe the manager/investor class intentionally sets out to shaft the workers. They get caught up in the competition of the marketplace, and just like any other resource, they cannot afford to 'overpay' the workforce (except the CEO, apparently).

Kevin Hallock, in a book called *Pay*[110], describes the process of Job Analysis that companies use to determine the right level of compensation for any given position. In a process analogous to Frederick Taylor's scientific management, each job is broken down into its simplest tasks, and each task evaluated relative to its importance to the company. The jobs are then ranked internally. Benchmark positions are established, and compared to those at competing companies (usually with information purchased from a compensation consulting firm). The whole idea for employers to go through this rigorous process is to find the exact right level of compensation that will allow them to hire competent workers <u>without paying them a penny more than necessary</u>.

This cold-hearted attitude can only exist when employers look at employees as costs to be contained, not as valued members of the clan. And with upper-level employers making the rules for lower-level employees, this will of course result in a perspective skewed in favor of the top of the organization. Apply this valuation process year after year and we get a compounded effect, and an increasing level of income inequality within each organization. Add the cronyism of corporate boards, and the problem is exacerbated throughout industries and the broader economy.

One remedy is to extend performance bonuses to employees at every level of the organization. In a column recommending just that, Michael Schuman spells out the reasons very clearly:

> *The root problem in today's corporate governance is the implicit assumption that only senior management and directors are responsible for a firm's success. Profits depend no less critically on the workers flipping burgers, stocking shelves or mopping the floors. Without them, the CEOs would have no company to run, and shareholders would have no profits to pocket.*[111]

Ryan Avent, in his book *The Wealth of Humans,* talks about the important role of communication within a corporation, describing it as the *social capital* of an organization:

> *The way that information flows within firms is hugely important to a company's performance. The ways that workers talk to each other, or decide what kinds of information to pass along to their bosses, makes the difference between success and failure. But that raises a critical issue: when most of a firm's economic value is tied up in the way its workers interact, just who should capture the lion's share of the profits when that firm succeeds?*[112]

Paycheck secrecy

Given the importance of communication within any organization, why do employers take such great pains to keep information about pay levels out of the hands of employees? The very essence of an efficient market depends upon a certain level of transparency, where both parties have some knowledge of the relative value, and the surplus and scarcity, of resources. That should be reflected in everyone's paycheck, information which would be of value to anyone working at the firm. So why are employees warned not to talk about their compensation with any other workers?

Pay scales are listed for entry level positions so the job applicant knows what to expect. But after that, all information about how much any given employee is paid is kept rather quiet. There are some exceptions. In the military for instance, a PFC can look up the salary of his company commander and first sergeant in the latest issue of *Army Times.* This may help explain why, in the most hierarchal organization possible, the compensation ratio of 4-star General to Private E-1 is 13:1; while in corporate America, the pay ratio of CEO to entry-level employee is 400:1.

Most places of employment are much more secretive about compensation packages than the military. Publicly traded companies are forced to release information on the five highest-paid employees (normally the CEO, the CFO, and three others). And there is a new rule, mandated by Dodd-Frank, that calls for the release of the ratio of the CEO's total compensation to that of the median compensation of its employees. (That ratio [median CEO to median worker] was 75:1 in 1979, and 175:1 in 2009.) These rules are meant to benefit the shareholders so they can be assured that not too much of a company's profits are directed to the compensation of company executives. But disclosure of these top salaries has not had a dampening effect in the past few decades. Quite the opposite. The compensation of the top five executives at large corporations has risen from 5 percent of total corporate income in 1993 to 15 percent in 2013![113]

We all seem to have a cultural aversion talking about our income and how much money we earn on the job. We have come to believe, somehow, that it's in bad taste – that it may seem like we are bragging about how wonderful we are. Or it could be that we are we afraid to talk about the salary we earn because we don't think we measure up to our peers, and are ashamed to admit it. In any event, we've had it drilled in our head that it's impolite for us to inquire how much others make, or vice versa.

Our employers love this reticence to discuss the subject. Indeed, they encourage our discretion, asking us that we not share with our co-workers when we get a raise because then they'll want a raise too. This is just one more way for the employer to have more power than the employee. He knows what everyone on the floor makes. The worker only knows how much he is paid.

Companies do announce periodic cost-of-living increases that are applied across the board to employees in good standing. But unless employed in a union shop or by the government, most employees spend their working lives not knowing how their specific salary measures up to their co-workers, much less their neighbors across the street. This ignorance leaves the employee greatly disadvantaged when it comes to negotiating his salary with his employer.

Parade magazine runs an annual *What People Earn* issue that publicizes the salaries of dozens of individuals, from entry-level workers to rock stars. The fact that these issues are read with such interest by so many folks should tell us something. This is more than just idle curiosity. Workers want to know if they are being paid fairly, and there is generally no easy way for them to find out.

A resourceful employee can dig up the information, of course. But many of us don't bother. I believe there are two reasons for that:

1. We do not measure our own self-worth strictly by the size of our paycheck.
2. We trust our employer to pay us fairly.
   (Unfortunately, that trust is sometimes not warranted.)

In an op-ed piece in Politico Magazine, Nick Hanauer, one of the fortunate early investors in *Amazon*, wrote a memo to *My Fellow Zillionaires*.[114] He writes:

> *the fundamental law of capitalism must be: If workers have more money, businesses have more customers. Which makes middle-class consumers, not rich businesspeople like us, the true job creators. Which means a thriving middle class is the source of American prosperity, not a consequence of it. The middle class creates us rich people, not the other way around.*

> *The thing about us businesspeople is that we love our customers rich and our employees poor.*
>
> *--Rich Hannauer*

Minimum wage laws

We need minimum wage laws for the same reason we need anti-littering laws. Some drivers are slobs. Some bosses are hogs. As Hanauer says, when a company pays their employees the minimum wage, what they are really saying is that they'd pay them even less if it were legal. And these business owners should know better. They should understand that the middle class has the potential to make them rich. Instead they subscribe to the *Us vs. Them* mentality when it comes to employer/employee relationship at their company. Hanauer writes:

> *In any large group, some people absolutely will not do the right thing. That's why our economy can only be safe and effective if it is governed by the same kinds of rules as, say, the transportation system, with its speed limits and stop signs.*

He goes on:

> *Capitalism, when well managed, is the greatest social technology ever invented to create prosperity in human societies. But capitalism left unchecked tends toward concentration and collapse. It can be managed either to benefit the few in the near term or the many in the long term.*

Minimum wage regulations are one example of how capitalism can be regulated to benefit the many, not just the few at the top.

Minnesota went a long time without adjusting the minimum wage, and for years was stuck at the Federal minimum of $7.25/hour. The state government finally got around to doing their job, and the minimum wage rose to $8.00/hour in August 2014, and $9.00/hour in August 2015, and to $9.50/hour in August 2016. Starting in 2018, the minimum wage will be tied to the rate of inflation, so no more abrupt changes should be necessary until the 40-hours-pay for 24-hours-work initiative passes.

The impact of minimum wage laws extends well beyond those earning just the minimum wage. In 2011, 36% of the job listings in Minnesota offered less than $10/hour. In 2015, just 13% of the listings fell in that same lowest category.[115] It seems very clear that Minnesota employers upped their opening wages on many jobs because of the impetus of the higher state minimum wage.

Historically, the Federal minimum wage hit its high point at $9.58/hour (in 2014 dollars) in 1968. In the 30 years preceding that point, it kept pace with gains in productivity fairly well. Since then, sadly, it has not even kept pace with inflation. The Economic Policy Institute calculated that the minimum wage should be over $18/hour at this time had it kept pace with gains in productivity.[116]

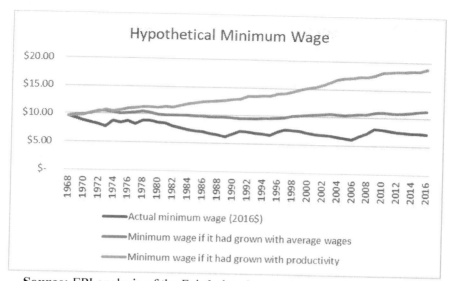

Source: EPI analysis of the Fair Labor Standards Act and amendments. Total economy productivity data from the Bureau of Labor Statistics Labor Productivity and Costs program. Average hourly wages of production nonsupervisory workers from the Bureau of Labor Statistics Current Employment Statistics.

If $18 an hour sounds like a lot of money to be paying an entry-level worker at a fast-food joint, consider this information from Robert Reich about who those workers are: in 2014, the median age for fast-food workers in the U.S. was 28, and the median age for workers in big-box retailers was over 30. These are not suburban teenagers looking to pick up some extra cash to buy the latest video game. More than a quarter of workers in those jobs have children, and they are major breadwinners for their families.

In Denmark, the same workers flip the same hamburgers at McDonalds as they do here, and they earn the equivalent of $20 an hour. The impact on the price of a Big Mac? A whopping 35¢ more than in the U.S. If the higher wages are not passed directly through to the consumer, they will *slightly reduce returns to shareholders and the compensation packages of top executives.* In a masterful understatement, Mr. Reich says *I do not find this especially troubling.*[117]

The abuse of salaried workers

For more proof that many employers cannot be trusted to do the right thing, we do not need to look at the very bottom of the pay scale. Look at the millions of salaried workers who receive no additional pay for working more than 40 hours a week (sometimes much more than 40 hours) while earning as little as $455/week (the current minimum for exempt status). If a convenience store shift manager is salaried at $480/week, he is making only $12.00/hour based on a 40-hour week (not exactly generous). But if he is putting in a 60-hour week, his effective pay is only $8.00/hour, not much over the federal minimum wage. This may be the person who is responsible for opening and closing the store, direct supervision of other employees, and handling the owner's money!

The salary threshold for employees exempt from OT pay was established to protect lower paid managers from just this sort of abuse. Yet employers have fought tooth-and-nail to keep that salary threshold as low as possible. And should a salaried employee demand too much of a raise, or grumble too much about anything else, his employer holds the ultimate trump card – the availability of the job itself.

Toward the end of the Obama administration, the President directed the DOL to raise the salary threshold up to $913/week with adjustments every three years based on inflation. Any salaried worker below this new higher level must be paid OT for all work beyond 40 hours/week.

That was in the summer of 2016. Business owners were not ready to give up this much ground without a fight, of course. A law suit and court injunction put the increase on hold while the legality of this move was sorted out. Now, under the Trump administration, DOL appears to be taking a much slower approach to this revision. There does seem to be general agreement that the old threshold of $455/week is "woefully inadequate". But as of this writing (Feb, 2018), it remains to be seen how far, if at all, the exempt threshold will rise.

Bumping the threshold up to $913/week would have impacted 5 million salaried workers who currently earn less than that and more than the old threshold of $455/week. These include convenience store managers, fast food shift-managers, and office workers. 56% are women, and 53% have college degrees. There is a very good chance they are the primary breadwinners for their families.

How can anyone argue these workers do not deserve to be paid for working overtime hours? Just think about this from the perspective of the spouse and children of the salaried worker. Why should there be no additional cost to the employer to keep the family breadwinner at work for hours on end with no additional pay? Why is the family not compensated for time lost at home?

Wage stagnation

Nationally, real wages have grown very little over the last 40 years despite steady growth in productivity all through that period. Robert Gordon lists several factors that account for the downward pressure on wages in his book *The Rise and Fall of American Growth,*: the decline in unionization, the rise in imports and immigration, automation, and the decline in the minimum wage.[118]

The following, copied from the Economic Policy Institute paper titled *Wage Stagnation in Nine Charts*, graphically tells the story:

Disconnect between productivity and typical worker's compensation, 1948–2013

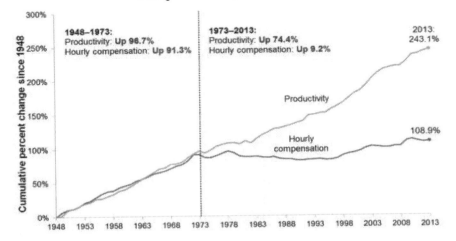

Note: Data are for compensation (wages and benefits) of production/nonsupervisory workers in the private sector and net productivity of the total economy. "Net productivity" is the growth of output of goods and services less depreciation per hour worked.
Source: EPI analysis of Bureau of Labor Statistics and Bureau of Economic Analysis data[119]

The authors go on to state:

> *Wage stagnation for the vast majority was not created by abstract economic trends. Rather, wages were suppressed by policy choices made on behalf of those with the most income, wealth, and power.*

The McKinsey Report *Technology, jobs, and the future of work* focuses on the 10-year period from 2005—14.

The vast majority of people derive incomes from jobs. In the United States, Western Europe, and across advanced economies, market incomes (from wages and capital) stagnated or fell for about two-thirds of households in 2005–14, a period marked by deep recession and slow recovery after the 2008 financial crisis. This was the first time incomes stopped advancing on such a scale since the stagflation era of the 1970s, and it may have helped stir popular opposition to globalization. The recession was a leading cause of the abrupt end to income advancement, but other longer-run factors also contributed, including a decline in the share of national income that is paid to workers, the so-called wage share. This has fallen across advanced economies despite rising productivity, suggesting a disconnect between productivity and incomes. The decline is due in part to the growth of corporate profits as a share of national income, rising capital returns to technology investments, lower returns to labor from increased trade, rising rent incomes from home ownership, and increased depreciation on capital.

A survey we conducted in France, the United Kingdom, and the United States showed an important proportion of those whose incomes stagnated are worried about their children's economic prospects—a sharp departure after many decades in which it was an article of faith that every generation would enjoy higher living standards than their parents. [120]

In *Saving Capitalism*, Robert Reich points out that corporations will even hold the threat of bankruptcy over employees as a way to keep wages down:

Over the last two decades, every major U.S. airline has been through bankruptcy at least once, usually in order to renege on previously agreed upon labor union contracts.

Under the bankruptcy code (again, largely crafted by credit card companies and bankers), labor contracts stipulating workers' pay have a relatively low priority when it comes to who gets paid off first. That means even the threat of bankruptcy can be a potent weapon for getting union members to sacrifice wages already agreed to. In 2003, American Airlines CEO Don Carty used such a threat to wring almost $2 billion of concessions from American's major unions. Carty preached the necessity of "shared sacrifice" but failed to disclose that he had secretly established a supplemental executive retirement plan whose assets, locked away in a trust, couldn't be touched in the event of bankruptcy. When Carty resigned he walked off with close to $12 million, courtesy of the secret plan.[121]

Summary

Employer vs. Employee? The proof is in the pudding, as they say. Employers take full advantage of all factors that keep their company's payroll down. Stagnating wages, despite strong productivity growth, demonstrate capitalism's *profits-über-alles* mentality, and confirm the adversarial nature of the employer vs. employee relationship.

CHAPTER 9

The Central Contradiction of the Labor Market

THOMAS PIKETTY'S *Capital in the Twenty-first Century* is a good place to start this chapter. The author looks at empirical data, going all the way back to 1700, of capital, production, income, and wealth inequality. Piketty concludes his monumental study with what he calls

The Central Contradiction of Capitalism:

$$r>g$$

Where **r** is the rate of return on capital, and **g** the rate of growth of income and output.[122]

What this boils down to is that it is easier to make money with money than with sweat and toil; and thus, *the rich get richer*. This principal applies to individual investors and to corporate entities alike. The implication then, is that strong companies will outperform weaker competitors, and that without some form of checks and balances, a process of attrition will continue, unobstructed, all the way to the point of monopolization.

Capitalism favors consolidation. David Korten goes so far as to call capitalism *the mortal enemy,* not just of ideal markets, but of democracy, and universal prosperity as well.[123] Korten notes that *market theory,* espoused by Adam Smith and many followers, only works with a number of specific conditions, including:

- Buyers and sellers must be too small to overly influence the market price.
- Complete information must be available to all participants. All trades are public.

In this day of oligopolistic markets, not only is neither condition satisfied, they are directly contradicted by present practices.

Robert Reich, in *Saving Capitalism,* writes that it is the combination of *unchecked economic and political power* that we need to guard against. He quotes Henry Demarest Lloyd from *Wealth Against Commonwealth* (1894):

> *The flames of the new economic evolution run around us, and we turn to find that competition has killed competition, that corporations are grown greater than the state . . . and that the naked issue of our time is with property becoming master, instead of servant.[124]*

Reich gives some examples of consolidation in how we use the internet today:

> *Despite an explosion of websites over the last decade, page views have become far more concentrated. While in 2001, the top ten websites accounted for 31 percent of all page views in America, by 2010 the top ten accounted for 75 percent.*

And Reich tells us that Amazon has become

> *the first stop for almost a third of American consumers who want to buy <u>anything</u>.*[125]

This consolidation of the internet is just one more example of **r>g**, and one more illustration of why businesses need oversight and regulation from governing bodies.

Monopoly is business at the end of its journey.

--Henry Demarest Lloyd

TURNING NOW TO THE LABOR MARKET, let me be so bold as to borrow the convention of Piketty's elegant inequality, and offer the following as an extension of that logic

The Central Contradiction of the Labor Market:

$$P_{employers} > P_{employees}$$

Where $P_{employers}$ is the power of the owner/manager class, and $P_{employees}$ the power of the worker class.

Substituting the terms Adam Smith sometimes used for employers and employees makes the formula even more self-evident:

$$P_{masters} > P_{servants}$$

This inequality holds true at all times, but is especially onerous for the working class when there is a surplus of labor and a scarcity of work. That is, during periods of high structural

187

unemployment – a condition repeatedly with us given the sensible application of new technology and capital to the production process.

The simple fact that the power of the owner/manager class is greater than the power of the workers should not be a surprise to anyone. But it is a question of degrees. To what extent is this imbalance true? Unfortunately, the employer already holds most of the cards, and this imbalance is becoming ever greater as the clear advantages of employing technology & capital continues to grow.

No worker can ever be confident that his job will be around forever. We spent Chapter 5 covering the tremendous impact of technology on the production process, and Chapter 6 talking about the global movement of production facilities. This places the owner/manager class clearly in the driver's seat when it comes to hiring workers. To make matters worse, employers are privy to the plans of the company, including the location of future production facilities, while employees are privy only to rumors. All of them scary. $P_{employers} > P_{employees}$.

Financialization

By December 2015, the recovery from the Great Recession seemed on solid footing. The Federal Reserve decided it was finally time to begin raising interest rates to calm fears of the inflation rate rising above around 2%. After all, 13 million jobs had been added since the depth of the recession, and the unemployment rate was down to around 5%. With those conditions, conventional wisdom says that wages should've been bounding upward. Harold Meyerson wrote an op-ed piece that questioned conventional wisdom and the Fed's action:

What the conventional theories failed to factor in is

power: the fact that workers have lost their ability to bargain with employers, the fact that major shareholders have gained the ability to compel corporate executives – often on penalty of losing their jobs – to funnel all available revenue to them. A cursory glance at – or in-depth survey of – U.S. business shows that companies are engaged in bargaining aplenty – not with their employees, however, who, with the rate of private-sector unionization reduced beneath 7 percent, have no means of bargaining. Rather, they're contending with "activist investors," who are reshaping the economic landscape by successfully pressuring companies to buy back their shares and merge with competitors, in the cause of enriching themselves. [126]

Meyerson's comments are spot-on. It is not possible for employers to put the welfare of their employees first with greedy shareholders and one-dimensional corporate boards interested only in profits earned in the last quarter, and it's not in their interest to put employees first when the decision makers (upper-level managers within the company) are rewarded solely on the basis of quarterly profits.

Given Piketty's finding that **r>g**, it is quite understandable that as successful corporations mature, they have a tendency to become hollowed-out holding companies. In a column that first appeared in the Washington Post, Guatum Mukunda tells us *What Bernie Sanders and Donald Trump get wrong about Wall Street.* [127] In a word, he calls it the *Financialization* of the economy. Mukunda writes:

> *The swollen financial sector misallocates capital by shifting investment from real assets (like factories) to financial ones, so company after company spends money buying their own stock instead of investing in the future. It misallocates talent by using status and money to lure*

people who would otherwise be creating value ... Think of all the brilliant engineers who work to shave milliseconds off high-frequency trades instead of actually generating wealth.

The role of finance is supposed to be supportive, to get capital to businesses for their operations when needed, and for business expansion when opportunities to grow are discovered.

There has always been a struggle between investors and operations, between short-term profits and long-term growth. But starting in the 1980's, the scale was tipped decidedly in favor of short-term profits. Some blame the corporate raiders with this shallow mindset. But the CEO's and the corporate boards were all too willing to go along with this single-minded pursuit as long as they were being so handsomely rewarded for their actions.

The result is inevitable. It leads to headlines that read like this: *Big pharmaceutical companies reluctant to produce Zika vaccine.* Reading the article, we learn that

> *For now, vaccine development seems like a risky venture for manufacturers that have recently taken part in a string of emerging diseases rodeos, from SARS and Ebola to the West Nile virus and the 2009 H1N1 pandemic. Those efforts have required significant investments on the part of major pharmaceutical companies, and have yielded either modest or no financial return.* [128]

From a purely financial standpoint, this reluctance to produce a new vaccine makes perfect sense. But these are pharmaceutical companies. Their core mission should be to develop drugs that make us healthier and safer. Bottom-line profits <u>should</u> be incidental to that. Therefore, small profits, and even just breaking-even should be acceptable as long as the company succeeds in eliminating the Zika virus as a threat to mankind. Shouldn't it?

The financial sector is supposed to serve the economy, not the other way around. Robert Reich points out that the $26 billion paid out as bonuses to Wall Street bankers would have been more than enough to double the salary of every one of America's 1 million full-time minimum wage workers. As Makunda puts it: *the tail of the economy is wagging the dog.*

Ryan Avent in *The Wealth of Humans* distinguishes between social capital and individual knowledge:

> *Social capital is individual knowledge that only has value in particular social contexts. ... But while social capital lives in the heads of people who make the economy go, its benefits flow disproportionately to the owners of financial capital. That mismatch is a source of significant economic trouble.* [129]

Our elected officials of both parties (including many Democrats, sad to say) too often ignore the value of a firm's collective *social capital*, and go along compliantly with the wishes of Wall Street. In the process, they become enablers of the inequality **r>g**, and by extension, $\mathbf{P_{employers}} > \mathbf{P_{employees}}$.

PAVLINA TCHERNEVA, an economist at Bard College, wrote a paper titled *When a Rising Tide Sinks Most Boats: Trends in US Income Inequality*. In it, she presents the chart and comments on the following page:

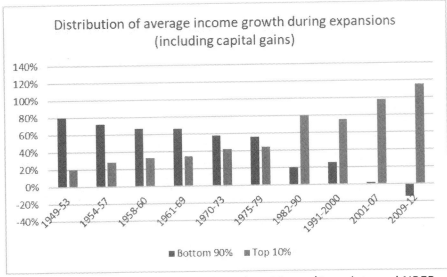

Distribution of average income growth during expansions
(including capital gains)

Bottom 90%   Top 10%

Sources: Tcherneva's calculations based on Piketty/Saez data and NBER

It turns out that in the postwar period, with every subsequent expansion, a smaller and smaller share of the gains in income growth have gone to the bottom 90 percent of families. Worse, in the latest expansion, while the economy has grown and average real income has recovered from its 2008 lows, all of the growth has gone to the wealthiest 10 percent of families, and the income of the bottom 90 percent has fallen. Most Americans have not felt that they have been part of the expansion. We have reached a situation where a rising tide sinks most boats.
130

The chart reflects the relative strength of labor unions and the middle class up through the 1970's. But there was a huge inflection point starting in the 1980's (the Reagan years – remember the Air Traffic Controllers union?), after which the top 10% of income earners have captured the lion's share of all growth. The middle and lower class had actually lost ground in the 2009-12 recovery.

WHAT HAS HAPPENED since 2012? By the end of Obama's second term, we finally started to see some real gains in middle class incomes, with about a 5% jump in the median household income in 2015. Noah Smith made these observations in November 2016 in a column for the Bloomberg View:

> *What's happening is a shift in who gets the money. Since 1980, growth has tended to benefit the rich a lot more than the middle class, and the middle class a bit more than the poor. In the last few years, that trend reversed. Though everyone gained, the poor and the middle class have done the best.*
>
> *Why is inequality falling, when for so long it seemed to go in only one direction? The short answer is that no one really knows.*[131]

I think I know. Political pressure to do <u>something</u> was building for some time. The *We are the 99%* and the *Occupy* movements date back to 2011. I believe the $15/hour minimum wage movement started on a very local basis in November 2013 with a vote in the town that encompasses the Seattle-Tacoma airport. From there it has spread to New York City, Washington DC, the state of California, and on to the middle of the country. The workers are finally gaining some political traction, but given the structure of commercial business in the modern world, it's going to be a long, up-hill battle.

Power concedes nothing without a demand. It never did and it never will.

--Frederick Douglass

Organizational theory

Corporations self-organize with boards of directors, a group of a dozen or so individuals, mostly senior business executives from outside the company, appointed to oversee the management of the company. The BOD is <u>supposed</u> to have fiduciary responsibilities to <u>all</u> stakeholders, not just the shareholders. As it turns out, the stockholders get the lion's share of the attention, and then some.

And how interested are the stockholders in anything other than quarterly dividends and earnings per share? We read in a column by Stephen Young titled *The realignment of the working class* that:

> *Most owners of stock (now dominated by large institutional funds) are essentially traders who "rent" the shares for a time hoping to "flip" them in a profitable sale to a new trader who in turn only hopes to flip them again.*[132]

Just as "absentee landlords" are sometimes not the best stewards of a neighborhood's housing stock, "absentee shareholders" pay little attention to operations of the corporation. All of us who own shares of mutual funds in 401(k) and 403(b) accounts are guilty of belonging to this absentee investor class.

For an example of how disinterest in anything other than short-term ROI can hurt a company in the long run, let's pick on Verizon since they were in the news fairly recently (in April 2016) with labor strikes up and down the east coast. Some 39,000 land line and cable employees walked off the job, complaining that they had been without a contract for eight months. No contract, although the company made a $17.9 billion profit in 2015, and paid out roughly half that amount in dividends to Verizon shareholders. That still left close to $9 billion that could've been used to sweeten the workers' paychecks. The company could've paid $10,000 profit-sharing bonuses to each striking worker, using 'just' $390 million of the profits. Is it possible that a bonus of that size would've kept all those striking workers off the picket line?

But, it appears to me, employees don't matter very much at Verizon. Scanning through 80-pages of their 2015 annual report reinforces my suspicion. Employees are barely mentioned except as liabilities in their severance and pension plans. At Verizon, just like at virtually every other large company, employees may be referred to as *human resources*, but they are treated as cost centers. Other than the star-power wages paid to the CEO and his immediate circle of friends, employees are paid "as much as it takes to attract the best talent". To phrase that another way, employees are paid "no more than absolutely necessary". Can you think of a better way to ensure that the employee <u>contributes</u> "no more than absolutely necessary"?

Corporate stakeholders

Let's imagine a situation where the corporate board of directors takes their fiduciary responsibilities seriously, and rewards the CEO based on a score that includes all six classes of company's stakeholders. Furthermore, let's imagine that the directors have seen the chart on page 182, and understand the need to make up for lost ground in employee wages over the last 45 years. We can well imagine, then, that the board would base the pay of the CEO according to how well he attends to the interests of all stakeholders, but in order of importance – employees first, shareholders last.

1. Employees
2. Customers
3. Suppliers
4. Community
5. Creditors
6. Shareholders

With this new scoring system in place, would we still have members of the S&P 500 using $98 out of every $100 of profit to pay dividends and to buy back stocks? Or might the CEO's begin to work a little harder to find ways to <u>grow</u> the company and to bring on <u>more</u> employees, instead of firing the workers already on-hand?

Some investors would rebel, and run to the companies that still placed the shareholders' pecuniary interests at the top of the list. But other investors would recognize the value of this mid-term approach, and reward the enlightened behavior with some patience of their own. Eventually, this broader, more humanistic approach to corporate governance would become the norm, and shares of stock in solid companies would still be the best long-term investment available.

A successful business maximizes the present value of future earnings.

--Stephen Young

International business regulation

The release of the *Panama Papers*[*] in the spring of 2016 created quite a stir. We learned a lot from these pilfered documents. As it turns out, there are hundreds of ways for wealthy individuals to hide their wealth and not pay taxes. Who knew?

And with wealthy families setting such a great example for

---

[*] A leak of 11 million financial records from the Panamanian law firm Mossack Fonseca to the International Consortium of Investigative Journalists (ICIJ)

the rest of us, is it any wonder that everyone from barbers to waiters don't report their tips, or that your plumber and auto mechanic will appreciate payments in cash? The OECD estimates that poor countries lose three times as much from tax evasion as they receive in foreign aid.[133]

Well, scofflaw individuals aren't the only ones hiding things from their government. Businesses are skilled at the practice of hiding income too. By claiming income is earned in faraway places (that just happen to have lower tax rates), they are, in effect, de-juicing the books back home.

Before the release of the Panama Papers, Gabriel Zucman came out with the cleverly titled *The Hidden Wealth of Nations*.[134] Zucman tells us that the birth of the tax haven can be traced back to Switzerland in the 1920s. Following WWI, wealthy families in France, Germany, and Italy began sending their fortunes to banks in Geneva, Zurich, and Basel. Nowadays, the tax haven 'industry' has extended well beyond simple numbered accounts in Swiss banks. Several countries are involved, and many investment instruments have been developed to hide income and wealth from governments with legitimate interests.

Zucman devotes a chapter to multinational corporations using tax havens to avoid paying taxes. Global corporations achieve this income-lowering sleight-of-hand by setting a low value on resources transferred from high-tax to low-tax jurisdictions, and a high value when transferring from low-tax to high-tax countries. Lower incomes mean lower taxes which means more profitability for the shareholders. Zucman's estimate is that these bookkeeping shenanigans cost just the U.S. $130 billion per year in lost tax revenue, not to mention all the other countries.

When multinational companies locate production facilities

overseas, there is generally a clear benefit to the local economy. When these same companies stash inordinate amounts of the wealth overseas, with the express purpose of avoiding taxes, that wealth has a much smaller impact on local economies. Case in point – Ireland. The GDP of Ireland grew an astounding 26.3% in 2015, up from a preliminary estimate of 7.8%.[135] Do you suppose the average Irish worker saw much of a benefit from that huge gain in GDP?

Ireland's corporate tax rate is 12.5%, one of the lowest in the developed world. And even there, loopholes abound. Apple, with its European HQ in Ireland, paid 0.005% on its European profits in 2014. All perfectly legal according to the rules established in Ireland.[136]

While the corporate lawyers at all these firms make sure these antics are legal, there is little regard to whether or not they are ethical. Clear evidence, in my opinion, that we cannot count on the free market to govern business practices. Some sort of systematic global accounting is needed, with the multinational companies held to a common standard of decency, perhaps akin to the Uniform Commercial Code (UCC) that U.S. companies abide by. Within this code of conduct would be the methodology to account for all income and all wealth on a global basis, then divvy it up country-by-country for taxing purposes. Zucman suggests using a formula that includes sales, salaries, and capital employed, each accounting for one-third, for allocating resources to individual countries. That seems reasonable.

One final thought here – is it possible that business enterprises are not just hiding income for the purpose of tax avoidance? Are they are hiding it from their own employees so that when it's time to negotiate labor contracts, they can point to empty cash drawers? (One more way for $P_{employers} > P_{employees}$.)

Moral capitalism

The Caux Round Table was established in 1986 as an international network of principled business leaders working to promote a moral capitalism. The organization has developed a thorough 7-point list as their *Principles for Responsible Business*. I include the entire list here because I agree with everything they stipulate a responsible business should do:

Principles for Responsible Business

PRINCIPLE 1 - RESPECT STAKEHOLDERS BEYOND SHAREHOLDERS

- A responsible business acknowledges its duty to contribute value to society through the wealth and employment it creates and the products and services it provides to consumers.
- A responsible business maintains its economic health and viability not just for shareholders, but also for other stakeholders.
- A responsible business respects the interests of, and acts with honesty and fairness towards, its customers, employees, suppliers, competitors, and the broader community.

PRINCIPLE 2 – CONTRIBUTE TO ECONOMIC, SOCIAL AND ENVIRONMENTAL DEVELOPMENT

- A responsible business recognizes that business cannot sustainably prosper in societies that are failing or lacking in economic development.
- A responsible business therefore contributes to the economic, social and environmental development of the communities in which it operates, in order to sustain its essential 'operating' capital – financial, social, environmental, and all forms of goodwill.
- A responsible business enhances society through effective and prudent use of resources, free and fair competition, and innovation in technology and business practices.

PRINCIPLE 3 – BUILD TRUST BY GOING BEYOND THE LETTER OF THE LAW

- A responsible business recognizes that some business behaviors, although legal, can nevertheless have adverse consequences for stakeholders.

- A responsible business therefore adheres to the spirit and intent behind the law, as well as the letter of the law, which requires conduct that goes beyond minimum legal obligations.
- A responsible business always operates with candor, truthfulness, and transparency, and keeps its promises.

PRINCIPLE 4 –RESPECT RULES AND CONVENTIONS

- A responsible business respects the local cultures and traditions in the communities in which it operates, consistent with fundamental principles of fairness and equality.
- A responsible business, everywhere it operates, respects all applicable national and international laws, regulations and conventions, while trading fairly and competitively.

PRINCIPLE 5 – SUPPORT RESPONSIBLE GLOBALISATION

- A responsible business, as a participant in the global marketplace, supports open and fair multilateral trade.
- A responsible business supports reform of domestic rules and regulations where they unreasonably hinder global commerce.

PRINCIPLE 6 – RESPECT THE ENVIRONMENT

- A responsible business protects and, where possible, improves the environment, and avoids wasteful use of resources.
- A responsible business ensures that its operations comply with best environmental management practices consistent with meeting the needs of today without compromising the needs of future generations.

PRINCIPLE 7 – AVOID ILLICIT ACTIVITIES

- A responsible business does not participate in, or condone, corrupt practices, bribery, money laundering, or other illicit activities.
- A responsible business does not participate in or facilitate transactions linked to or supporting terrorist activities, drug trafficking or any other illicit activity.
- A responsible business actively supports the reduction and prevention of all such illegal and illicit activities.[137]

Members of the Caux Round Table believe in *Moral Capitalism*: that the purpose of business is to serve society, and that profit is the reward for serving society well. This is high-minded stuff! If only all companies could be convinced to adopt these principles, the world would be a far better place.

If only. Looking back at the history of the Caux Round Table, we see that the organization was led through most of the 1990s by Winston Wallin, the chairman at Medtronic. Medtronic is the huge medical device company that acquired the Irish company Covidien in January 2015, and promptly moved their corporate headquarters to Dublin, keeping operational headquarters in Fridley, Minnesota. While the product lines and technical strength of $17 B Medtronic and $10 B Covidien are arguably quite complementary, and justify the merger of these two medical giants, moving the corporate HQ to Ireland can hardly be justified by any motive other than tax-inversion.

Moral capitalism and tax avoidance. Cognitive dissonance anyone?

Make all employees owners

A sensible solution to the *Central Contradiction of the Labor Market* would be to make all employees owners of the enterprise. Give everyone who works at a business a stake in the outcome. Some employees contribute more than others, and some are more exposed to downside risks. Ownership should be allocated accordingly. But all employees who contribute to the success of the operation would share in the profits when things are going well, and be willing to forego any bonuses when times are tough.

This should be more than awarding just a few token shares to an ESOP plan in an effort of appeasement. Employees will know the difference between real commitment to the principal of shared profits and the equivalent of 'financial lip service' from management.

This topic was covered nicely by authors David Madland and Karla Walter in a paper titled *Growing the Wealth*. They offer several approaches to *inclusive capitalism*[138], including everything from full-blown co-ops to periodic profit-sharing. Another resource is from Jeff Gates in his book *The Ownership Solution*.[139] Gates tells us that *capitalism embodies a curious and dangerous inconsistency*. The system contains lots of capital, but few capitalists – with the lopsided share of corporate ownership resting with the top 1%. Gates writes:

> *Today's detached and disconnected capitalism is now largely "on automatic," with investment decisions based on a "by the numbers" process that is incapable of taking into account many longer-term concerns, including the impact those investments have on the social fabric, on the fiscal condition of the nation, and on the environment.*[140]

Coming back to the Caux Round Table, we find their stakeholder guidelines regarding **Employees**:

A responsible business treats every employee with dignity and respects their interests. Business therefore has a responsibility to:

a. Provide jobs and compensation that contribute to improved living standards
b. Provide working conditions that protect each employee's health and safety.
c. Provide working conditions that enhance each employee's well-being as citizens, family members, and capable and caring individuals
d. Be open and honest with employees in sharing information, limited only by legal and competitive constraints.
e. Listen to employees and act in good faith on employee complaints and issues.
f. Avoid discriminatory practices and provide equal treatment, opportunity and pay in areas such as gender, age, race, and religion.
g. Support the employment of differently-abled people in places of work where they can be productive.
h. Encourage and assist all employees in developing relevant skills and knowledge.

i. Be sensitive to the impacts of unemployment and work with governments, employee groups and other agencies in addressing any employee dislocations.

j. Ensure that all executive compensation and incentives further the achievement of long- term wealth creation, reward prudent risk management, and discourage excessive risk taking.

k. Avoid illicit or abusive child labor practices.[141]

This *moral capitalism* sure sounds good on paper. What's missing? *Employee ownership* – a chance for the workers to share in the wealth they have created.

Giving workers a stake in the operation is strategically smart. In a column on employee retention, business consultant Harvey McKay writes that *Solving employee turnover is easier when they own a piece of the pie.*[142] This will be true during periods of strong and weak labor markets.

Classes of employees

Perhaps we need a new way of classifying employers and employees, and I offer the following not as a firm proposal, but as a concept to think about: A first-tier worker would indicate full ownership, one who shares fully in both risks and rewards. The equivalent of today's entrepreneur, or a full partner in a law firm. A second-tier worker would indicate one who shares in a substantial portion of the profits of the organization, but is not exposed to the downside risks. The equivalent to many employees at profit sharing companies today. A third-tier worker would indicate a person who works for his paycheck only. No profit sharing. No benefits. The equivalent to many part-time workers and contract workers today.

The 24-hour workweek mandate would apply most directly to third tier workers, not at all to first tier workers, and with some flexibility to second tier workers.

A case could be made to allow seasonal workers into the second tier. This would allow agricultural workers to work around the clock, making hay when the sun shines. The overtime pay mandate need not kick in IF the profits tier-two workers share from the sale of the hay more than make up the difference from the lost overtime.

This would put a whole new spin on the value of a seasonal worker. Forcing the farmer to classify a seasonal worker as second or third tier would force the owners to acknowledge the value of those workers.

Will this be a bucketful of headaches for business owners? Perhaps initially. But if the rules apply to every business in every industry, we have a level playing field. An in-depth study of *inclusive capitalism* and the ramifications of the various approaches to employee ownership is beyond the scope of this book. Let me just close this chapter with a quote that every conservative should love from a great liberal statesman, Hubert H. Humphrey:

> *... capital and the question of who owns it and therefore reaps the benefit of its productiveness, is an extremely important issue that is complementary to the issue of full employment. ... I see these as the twin pillars of our economy: Full employment of our labor resources and widespread ownership of our capital resources. Such twin pillars would go a long way in providing a firm underlying support for future economic growth that would be equitably shared.*[143]

Economics is not a zero-sum game. Collectively, we will all be better off at the close of the business day if the workers share in the profits of the organization.

CHAPTER 10

Working Out of Poverty with a Mandated 24-hour Workweek

RECALIBRATE THE LABOR MARKET. That's quite an ambitious goal. Is it even possible to calibrate, much less recalibrate, a living, breathing, economic entity like a market? History tells us yes. The U.S. Congress, along with a strong push from President Franklin Delano Roosevelt, enacted the Fair Labor Standards Act in 1938. That law includes the requirement to pay employees overtime for all work greater than 40-hours/week. With that mandate, 40-hours became the de facto standard for a fulltime workweek for all industries, not just in America but around the globe. Amending the FLSA to officially establish 24-hours as a fulltime job should have the same impact today.

Why 24?

Moving from a 40- to a 24-hour workweek will be a BIG disruption to the labor market. Why 24 hours/week? Well, not to be too flip, why not? 40 is an arbitrary number. So is 24. And we are trying to mend a labor market that is seriously out-of-balance, so no tinkering around the edges here. We need a substantial change – one that is 80 years overdue. The last major adjustment to the workweek took place over a 50-year span from the 1880s to the 1930s. We went from six 10-hour days to five 8-hour days, from 60 hours to 40 hours a week. That is a 33% drop in hours worked. Moving now from 40- to 24-hours of work per week is a 40% drop, in line with the last major adjustment a century ago.

And 24 hours a week is <u>so handy</u>! It's being on-the-clock one full day every week.

Number of days worked per week	Hours on the clock each work day
1	24
2	12
3	8
4	6
5	4.8
6	4
7	3.42857142857142857142857

What could be easier than that? Especially if you are one of those indispensable assets needed at work 7-days a week.

If (nay – <u>when</u>) the 24-hour workweek becomes the law of the land, the length of everyone's workweek will quickly cluster around that point. Look at the graph on the next page showing the length of the workweek for American workers in 2012, this with the 40-hour workweek in effect:

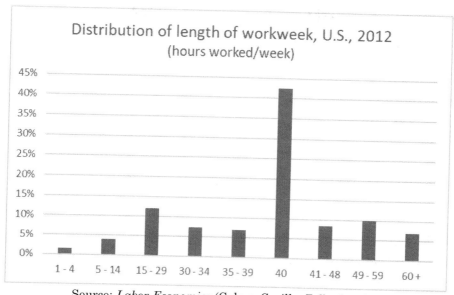

Distribution of length of workweek, U.S., 2012
(hours worked/week)

Source: *Labor Economics* (Cahuc, Carillo, Zylberberg)

Note that over 40% put in exactly 40 hours a week, and that almost as many workers put in more than 40 hours a week (25%) as work less (32%). This chart covers both salaried and hourly workers. We can assume that most of those working well over 40 hours a week are salaried (employers don't like paying overtime). We can also assume that a fair number of those who list 40 hours are salaried. They probably work more than 40 hours some weeks, less on others, and they say they average 40 hours a week because that is the standard fulltime job.

With a 24-hour workweek in effect, the whole distribution will shift to the left, with a strong spike at the 24-hour mark.

The important thing to remember is that there will be a corresponding gain of leisure time each week for almost all these workers. That has the potential of being tremendously beneficial for society. (Please see Chapter 4.)

Managing the Change

In Daniel Hamermesh's study *Workdays, Workhours and Work Schedules*, he states that one lesson learned from his in-depth comparison of workweek schedules in the U.S. and Germany in 1990-91 is:

> *The detrimental side-effects from cutting the workweek to stimulate employment demand may be smaller if cuts in daily hours are mandated than if employers are required to reduce the number of workdays.* [144]

In other words, we'd be more productive, week-by-week, working several short days than fewer long days. This would seem to jive with the Monday-morning period of non-productivity many of us experience, as well as the daily burn-out we often feel as the afternoon wears on. But in each industry, we'll need to find a balance between what's good for the employer and the employee. Which will be the most efficient 24-hour workweek will vary from industry to industry; from company to company; and just as importantly, from employee to employee. Finding the optimal combination will call for some creative experimentation. Remember that the 24-hour part is mandated – all companies will be faced with the same scheduling challenges. The companies that rise to the top will arguably be the healthiest and best-managed. In a competitive, capitalist marketplace, this is the best outcome we can hope for.

If three 8-hour days becomes the standard, that may mean a workweek of M-T-W for one worker, and Th-F-Sa for the next. In other situations, maybe M-W-F and T-Th-Sa system of job-sharing would work better. This should be determined by the preferences of <u>both</u> employers and employees.

The psychiatrist Adolf Meyer, an early practitioner of occupational therapy, encouraged us long ago to strike a balance between work, play, and rest.[145] When a workaholic puts in an

80-hour week, that doesn't sound like a healthy balance. Nor does the unemployed person with no work at all. What is the right amount of work? It may have been 60 hours a week in the year Meyer was born (1866). I believe it's closer to 24 hours a week today.

Rutger Bregman writes: *The purpose of a shorter workweek is not so we can sit around all day doing nothing, but so we can spend more time on the things that really matter to us.* [146] From my perspective, working 24 hours a week instead of 40, and freeing up 16 hours a week to divvy up among activities of our own choice *feels* like a healthy place to be.

Most people want to be contributing members of the community. Working 24 hours a week will give them greater opportunities to do so outside the workplace. And reducing the length of the workweek will open up slots for more people to join the workforce.

Labor Economics 101

Economists tell us that the labor market responds to changes just as all markets do, and can be modeled with classic supply & demand curves. The shape of these curves will be influenced by the decisions of three groups of actors: employees (labor supply), employers (labor demand), and the government (e.g. by mandating the length of the standard workweek).[147] Labor Supply, the number of workers willing to work at any given wage, will slope upward as wages rise. Labor Demand, the number of workers that firms want to hire, slopes downward as wages rise.

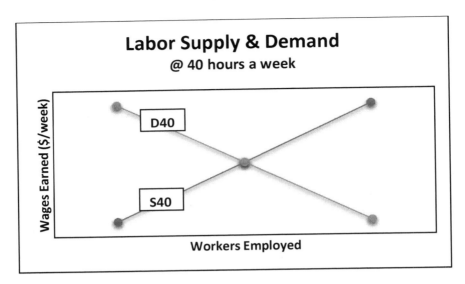

At any point in time and in any given situation, there will be a point of Equilibrium, where the Labor Supply (S40) and Demand (D40) curves cross. The market is theoretically optimized at this point, with the fewest number of individuals who want to work without a job and the fewest number of unfilled positions in hiring firms. The Equilibrium Point in America today is around 124 million fulltime jobs (> 35 hrs/week), and a wage around $800/week (close to the median income in the country).

But what would happen if the government stepped in and changed the rules in the Labor Market? What would happen if the government mandated that workers earn as much after 24 hours of work as they now earn in 40 hours/week, and that no employee can put in more than 24 hours a week with one employer without being paid overtime?

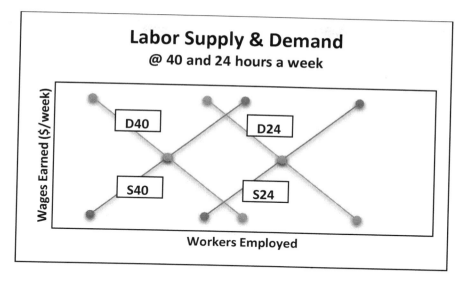

The new Supply curve (S24) would shift to the right as more people would be willing to put in a 3-day workweek to earn $800 than had been the case with a 5-day workweek. And here's the real game-changer: The new Demand curve (D24) would be <u>forced</u> to the right as employers would have to hire more 24-hour/week workers to keep their factories producing at the same level and their shops open the same number of hours. And there will be workers available to fill those positions because their first fulltime job is now just 24 hours/week. One worker can now hold down two fulltime jobs if he desires, or if needed. The median wage of a single fulltime job should stay right around $800/week, but there would be many more individuals employed. And now, the worker who holds down two jobs to support his family will still be able to spend some time with his family.

How many more jobs will this create? This question is best left to economists. This much we know: The number of fulltime workers is now close to 124 M, and part time workers 28 M, so around 152 M paid jobs in the U.S. all told. If we simply multiplied these totals by the ratio 40/24, we would end up with

207 M fulltime and 46 M part time positions.

But there's a very good chance that will not happen. Under the heading 'unintended consequences', as the cost of labor increases, employers will accelerate the move to automation and robotics.* Some jobs will become as productive in 24 hours as they had been in 40. Other jobs will be eliminated altogether. And as we saw back in Chapter 5, the jobs at risk are no longer limited to simple assembly tasks (the technological equivalent of 'low-hanging fruit'). Artificial Intelligence is now reaching into the offices of American businesses, eliminating the need for many jobs once thought of as secure.

Again, I'll leave it to the experts to forecast how many workers will be available to accept jobs (Supply) and how many new positions employers will add (Demand). I am confident that the total number of jobs will be significantly higher than the 152 M today. But the only way to assure this happens is to mandate changes to the labor market.

Why mandated?

The city of Gothenburg, Sweden ran a two year experiment with a 30-hour workweek (five 6-hour workdays) at a municipal retirement home. From the workers' perspective, it was quite a success, as the shorter working hours led to *happier, healthier, and more productive employees.*[148] The city paid the workers the same amount for their 6-hour day as they had paid for 8-hours. The workers loved it. Their immediate supervisors loved it. But the city pulled the plug on the experiment.

I don't know this to be the case, but I'm guessing the decision to

---

* In truth, there is nothing 'unintended' about these consequences as far as I'm concerned. Let the machines do the grunt work!

terminate the experiment was more political than financial or operational. You see, the whole city of Gothenburg wasn't on the 6-hour schedule. Just the retirement home and a handful of private businesses (including a Toyota maintenance facility – still on the shorter workweek). There must've been a fair amount of envy in the air, and that would've resulted in political squabbling and pressure to return to the status quo. This illustrates why the change needs to be mandated for all industries, and throughout any political jurisdiction.

And why not voluntary? Because capitalists get greedy. Stephan Young puts this very succinctly in his book *Moral Capitalism:*

> *Humanity is better off with markets and capitalism than with poverty and feudalism. Yet markets and capitalism facilitate abuse of the very power they create. For all the inherent preferences of markets for high levels of trust and reliability, for all the social good they can wring from individual pursuit of self-interest, capitalist markets have no cure for the hardness hiding in many human hearts.* [149]

CERTIFIED FINANCIAL PLANNERS

In April 2016, the Department of Labor issued a ruling that Certified Financial Planners must first honor their fiduciary duties to their clients before considering their own well-being. This ruling caught me by surprise. Like a lot of American investors, I had assumed this was always the case.

While this has nothing to do with the 24-houor workweek, it does reinforce why we need rules and regulations governing our economic transactions.

Robert Reich offers an explanation of the need for rules in his summary of market mechanisms:

Markets are made by human beings—just as nations, governments, laws, corporations, and baseball are the products of human beings. And as with these other systems, there are many alternative ways markets can be organized. However organized, the rules of a market create incentives for people. Ideally, they motivate people to work and collaborate, to be productive and inventive; they help people to achieve the lives they seek. The rules will also reflect their moral values and judgments about what is good and worthy and what is fair. The rules are not static; they change over time, we hope in ways that most participants consider to be better and fairer.[150]

Who makes the rules? The government makes the rules. As Reich tells us, this has nothing to do with the size or "intrusiveness" of government. Legislatures, government agencies, and the courts – all are needed to make the rules. And ideally, the rules are made with the objective of providing the greatest good to the greatest number of citizens.

Government doesn't "intrude" on the "free market". It creates the market.

--Robert Reich

151

All these rule makers are susceptible to outside influence – from large corporations and wealthy individuals on the one side, and from labor unions on the other. Elected officials count on those with deep pockets for donations for their reelection campaigns. Many agency officials benefit from revolving-door work opportunities at the very institutions they are charged with regulating. Those in the judiciary are theoretically least susceptible to outside pressure, but their rulings sometimes cause one to wonder.

What we end up with is a vicious cycle – those with dominant economic power have the greatest influence over the rule makers, and this perpetuates the status quo or moves the market more in favor of the current beneficiaries. Reich tells us this could, and should, be replaced with a virtuous cycle:

> *in which widely shared prosperity generates more inclusive political institutions, which in turn organize the market in ways that further broaden the gains from growth and expanded opportunity.* [152]

Let's bring all this back to the labor market: In chapter 8, I wrote about the abuse of low-paid salaried workers, and the need for rules governing the payment of overtime. With no update to the rule, employers can classify salaried workers earning as little as $23,660 a year as 'exempt' from OT rules. The update that the Obama administration proposed would have extended OT protection to 4 million workers.

As salaried workers, some of these hapless employees are expected to put in 50 – 60 hour workweeks and more. It's one thing to put in long hours when you directly benefit from the effort (like the owner of a franchise). It's quite another when you are working for less than $30,000/year and you never get to see your family because the boss expects you at work morning, noon, and night.

King Banaian, an economics professor at St. Cloud State, wrote a column questioning the wisdom of applying the new overtime rules to publishing assists, assistant coaches, sous-chefs, and post-doc students – new workers on their way to learning a trade and working their way into very lucrative careers. He wrote that *every employer and employee are the best judges of what their relationship should be*.[153] In an ideal world, he's right. And an ideal world would have no need for child labor laws, a minimum wage, or OSHA regulations.

The regulations regarding overtime are needed because some employers are unscrupulous, pure-and-simple. They take advantage of the enthusiasm of young workers eager to learn the ropes. I see parallels with here with unpaid internships. A lot of these mostly young workers are striving to learn on the job and work their way into lucrative careers at the same time they are just starting to raise young families. The only ones who will be able to work for peanuts and not suffer undue economic hardship are those from wealthier families. All the rest need a living wage.

We can see the unfortunate impact of unpaid internships: The college graduates already strapped with huge debts from student loans will just go deeper in debt with another year of unpaid work, and will struggle for years to pull themselves out of debt. Income inequality in the U.S. will continue to grow.

Lower pay for new employees engaged in on-the-job-training is justified. But unpaid internships? No. There is no justification for that.

Companies large and small, for-profit and not-for-profit, will all have pages on their websites proclaiming that their employees are their most valuable assets. But despite the tripe you read on HR webpages, most companies do not place the welfare of their workers at the very top of their priority lists. (If they did, I wouldn't be writing this book.) They treat workers as resources, and like all other resources, they are employed as expeditiously as possible. That means paying no more than necessary for salaries and benefits.

Slavery

This treatment of workers, as economic resources and not human beings, is hardly a new phenomenon. Let's go back to *Uncle Tom's Cabin* for a historical perspective. One of the main characters in Harriet Beecher Stowe's classic work is Augustine St. Clare, a slave-holder in New Orleans who is uncomfortable in that role, but is unable to see a way to do things better. Augustine's cousin Ophelia from Vermont comes south to help manage the St. Clare household. Ms. Ophelia, along with most of her northern neighbors, is openly anti-slavery. Augustine and Ophelia are always arguing about the relative evils of slavery. Augustine acknowledges problems with the institution:

> *Tell me that any man living wants to work all his days, from day-dawn to dark, under the constant eye of the master, ... on the same dreary, monotonous, unchanging toil. ... Any man who thinks that human beings can, as a general thing, be made about as comfortable that way as any other, I wish he might try it.*

He goes on, *the American planter is only doing, in another form, what the English aristocracy and capitalists are doing by the lower classes; that is ... appropriating them, body and bone, soul and spirit, to their use and convenience.*

Ophelia counters, *How in the world can the two things be compared? The English laborer is not sold, traded, parted from his family, whipped.*

Augustine replies that the English laborer *is as much at the will of his employer as if he were sold to him. The slave-owner can whip his refractory slave to death, -- the capitalist can starve him to death. As to family security, it is hard to say which is worst, -- to have one's children sold, or to see them starve to death at home.* [154]

With these vivid thoughts and images in mind, we have to wonder – would we still have the institution of slavery in Louisiana were it not for government intervention from President Lincoln and the Union States? Would this still be an accepted practice in the southern states without the coercive action taken by the U.S. government? Imagine the status of labor relations in the Confederate States without Lincoln's Emancipation Proclamation, without the defeat of the Confederate army by the Union troops, and without the passage and ratification of the 13th Amendment in 1865. The abolition of slavery required the passage of *enforceable* laws by the U.S. government.

Richard Donkin, in his book *Blood, Sweat & Tears,* quotes Adam Smith from the *Wealth of Nations*:

> *It appears from the experience of all ages and nations, that work done by free men comes cheaper in the end than that performed by slaves.* [155]

While I can't argue with Smith's observation, I am quite sure that it was human decency, not economics, that ultimately led to the abolition of slavery. Abraham Lincoln was motivated by human decency, not economics.

Child labor laws

The need for child labor laws further prove that the 24-hour workweek must be mandated. These laws, which started in England, spread quickly to the Continent and to America.

It is now so universally accepted that children are not expected to work that we forget this was not always the case. In fact, it is a relatively recent development. Throughout most of recorded history, children worked side-by-side with their parents. In the agricultural age, farming was a family-based and community-based activity. Farm families had lots of kids, not so they'd have more mouths to feed, but more hands to work in the fields and tend to the animals. Then, as now, everyone on the farm had chores, with the children expected to put in full days just like mom and dad.

Other children were employed as servants, most likely in service to the same aristocratic families as their parents. As the boys got a little older, they may have been apprenticed to tradesmen or craftsmen in the community. With the children working with or near their parents, it was easy enough for families to keep an eye on things and make sure their offspring were being brought up properly and not being abused.

The industrial revolution changed these cozy arrangements. With the development of larger factories, adults and children from many families and different communities were brought together under one roof to manufacture goods for the factory owners. Most of this work was physical in nature. While adults were hired for their strength and stamina, children were prized for their small size and nimble hands. Factory owners paid all the workers as little as possible, of course. And they paid the women and children less, justifying this because they were smaller and weaker.

In these larger manufacturing plants, the children became cogs in the machinery, just like their parents. And in the larger plants, the children may not have been working within eyesight of their parents, and the chances for abuse would be even greater.

But the parents of working children had little recourse until the hue and cry from the families reached the point where it could not be ignored by the political establishment. And it wasn't until the passage of child labor laws that protection for the children was codified. From England, these laws propagated to the Continent and to the Americas.

The operative word, again, is *laws*. Without legal mandates, the manufacturers in Europe and North America would have continued to use children as laborers in their factories.

Absentee owners

We like to think that we are far more enlightened nowadays regarding the abuse of workers than were the plantation owners and sweatshop operators of the mid-nineteenth century. And I believe that we are. But there is a countervailing trend that leaves the welfare of workers still very much in doubt. That trend is absentee ownership of corporations.

The slaveholder would hire a master to deal with the slaves directly, but he still frequently had occasion to rub elbows with the domestic servants and the field hands – to look them in the eye. But what is the likelihood that the owners of a large corporation today would recognize any worker at that corporation? Not too likely – not when you realize the owners are you, me, and a million other mutual fund shareholders.

The shareholders are not concerned about the workers. Nor, in many cases, is company management (as discussed in Chapter 8). Nor the customers who buy the company's products (see Chapter 3). So, who does have the welfare of the workers at heart?

Labor unions did at one time, but the influence of unions has declined precipitously. As we mentioned earlier, General Motors was once the country's largest private employer. Today, it is Walmart.

Just as we needed the government to step in and establish child labor laws, we need the government to make changes that are needed today. We should amend the FLSA to read 24-hours/week instead of 40. That will push the balance of power in the labor market back in toward the employees. Employers will still be able to make the calls, but at least the imbalance in $P_{employers} > P_{employees}$ will not be as large. If we start in the U.S., other nations will quickly follow suit.

24 hours of labor must yield a 40-hour paycheck

A worker whose hours are cut from 40 to 24 hours a week must not suffer any lost income. The cleanest way to accomplish this for an hourly worker is for the employer to give the employee an immediate pay raise of 67% (e.g. from $20/hour to $33.33/hour). While that proposal sounds ridiculously impossible for any single company, it should not create a problem if all companies are faced with the same challenge, and we have a level playing field.

Salaried workers and their employers can either opt for a comparable bump in pay, or just agree to back off on the number of hours they put in at work by at least 40% (e.g. from 60 hours a week to 36). Language to assure these changes in compensation are implemented should be included in the amended FLSA.

In a column by Minnesota politician John Marty, we learn that in national poll in 2000, an overwhelming 94% of Americans agreed with the principle that "people who work full time should

---

People who work full time should earn enough to keep their families out of poverty.

---

be able to earn enough keep their families out of poverty".[156] Hopefully that's the reason why, 15 years later, the push for a $15 minimum wage is gaining steam all across the country.

The poverty threshold is set by the U.S. Census Bureau, using a figure three times the cost of a minimum food diet. It is constantly updated to account for inflation. The chart below shows some interesting trends in the rates of poverty.[157]

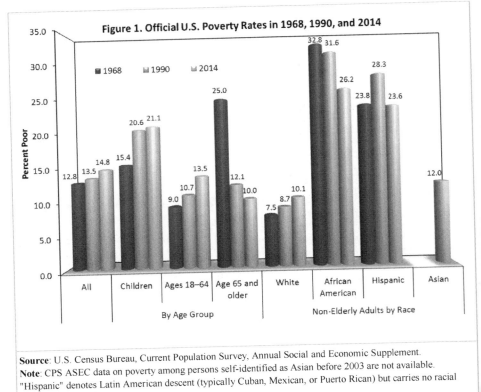

Figure 1. Official U.S. Poverty Rates in 1968, 1990, and 2014

Source: U.S. Census Bureau, Current Population Survey, Annual Social and Economic Supplement.
Note: CPS ASEC data on poverty among persons self-identified as Asian before 2003 are not available. "Hispanic" denotes Latin American descent (typically Cuban, Mexican, or Puerto Rican) but carries no racial designation.

The most noticeable single comparison is the drop in the poverty rate for those age 65 and older from 25 to 12% between 1968 and 1990 (thanks AARP!). Unfortunately, it looks like a lot of those gains were at the expense of children. Poverty rates for

African Americans are dropping, while those for whites are rising, but there are still 2½ times more blacks than whites living in poverty. Overall, poverty rates have risen from near 13% to near 15% over these two generations. How can this be possible when the GPD grew almost 4X over that same period? Do you suppose this has anything to do with CEO pay rising 1500% over those 46 years, while workers' compensation has increased by 40%? How many people <u>with</u> fulltime jobs are living in poverty?

One possible remedy to the excessive compensation packages is to tie the corporate tax rate to the ratio of

---

In 1968 the average CEO made 20 times the average worker's pay.

Today that multiple is closer to 400 times.

---

compensation of the CEO to the median worker in the company. Tax policy could also be used to encourage pay raises for those average employees, perhaps tied to the company's growth in productivity, or to the broader growth in the state economy.

Working out of poverty

The 2016 U.S. poverty thresholds for families of different sizes are shown on the following page:[158]

2016 POVERTY GUIDELINES FOR THE 48 CONTIGUOUS STATES AND THE DISTRICT OF COLUMBIA	
PERSONS IN FAMILY/HOUSEHOLD	POVERTY GUIDELINE
1	$11,880
2	$16,020
3	$20,160
4	$24,300
5	$28,440
6	$32,580
7	$36,730
8	$40,890
For families/households with more than 8 persons, add $4,160 for each additional person.	

Let's take a look at some mechanisms, used in conjunction with the 24-hour workweek, to allow the working poor to work their way out of poverty:

Minimum wage

If the minimum wage was set at $15/hour and a worker put in a fulltime 24-hour week, he would earn $360/week, $18,720/year. That will keep himself and his wife just above the poverty threshold. But if they have children, they fall below the line. It looks like $20/hour is a better mark for the minimum wage in conjunction with the 24-hour workweek. That yields an annual salary of $24,960, just enough for the income from one fulltime job to reach the poverty threshold for a family of four, two adults and two children.

That still leaves this family of four living in poverty, and most will not be satisfied with that. For those couples who want to get rid of their debt and crawl out of the trap of poverty, the 24-hour workweek makes it much easier for the wife to hold a fulltime job opposite her husband. She could work M-T-W, while he works Th-F-S; or she in the mornings and he in the evenings. With two fulltime minimum wage jobs, and no child-care expenses, the family earning around $50K/year has an income we now consider middle class. And that is where working-class families should reside – firmly in the middle class.

Many families will not be satisfied with that, and will be driven to do even more. With 24-hour a week employment, they have more free time to commit to second, third, and even fourth fulltime jobs, or possibly time to devote to a home business. Four fulltime jobs (96 hours/week for the household) at $20/hour yields close to $100k/year. Quite respectable.

Working-class families should not be living in poverty. A $20/hour minimum wage in conjunction with a 24-hour workweek sounds quite sensible.

Earned Income Tax Credit

If private companies tell us a $20/hour minimum wage is impossible, we do have an alternative. We can let the government make up the difference between a low-wage job and a living-wage income. We already have a tax law in place to supplement low-income work – the *Earned Income Tax Credit*. What is needed is a mechanism to assure that the worker receives the EITC as it is earned, paycheck by paycheck. Republicans love the EITC because it rewards work, not inactivity. (It also just happens to be, in effect, a huge subsidy for businesses, large and small. It allows them to keep their payroll as low as possible without all that guilt.)

The EITC could have a very positive effect on short and intermediate-term labor demand, with the bigger the credit, the greater the effect. We can draw a simple graph using $20/hour as the standard:

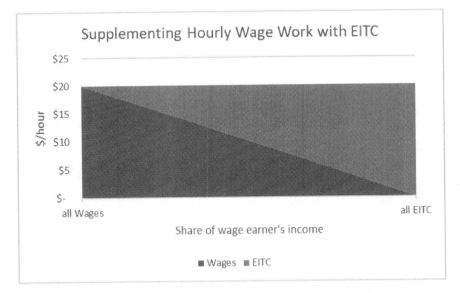

Compensation for the employees can all come out of the employer's operational budget as wages, or all from the taxpayers, or somewhere in between. Greater amounts from EITC and less from the employer should slow down the elimination of jobs via outsourcing or automation. The EITC is a tax incentive to employ labor when it might otherwise by prudent to employ capital. With that in mind, maybe we need a $10/hour minimum wage paired with a matching $10/hour EITC? The key would be that all $20/hour is received by the worker on payday.

Whatever the share of EITC to wages, the government should put a cap on the amount of EITC any individual could earn. Remember that one of the primary motivations for the 24-hour workweek is to reduce the level of unemployment. Therefore, the EITC should be capped at 24 hours a week. This, of course, would not prevent anyone from working a second job at $10/hour, and certainly wouldn't slow him down from accepting a $20/hour position.

The EITC may just be a stop-gap measure. Low paying jobs will continue to disappear, and we may well reach the point where, even with the EITC supplement, it will be impossible for employers to hold jobs open for human workers when there are many more efficient options available. That brings us to the next alternative.

Unconditional Basic Income

Another option for government intervention would be an *unconditional basic income* for all adult residents. This has the advantage of assuring that everyone, working or not, receives a basic level of income. It has the disadvantage of de-linking economic assistance to work, breaking the connection between receiving benefits from society and the effort we put forth in the manner of paid work to benefit society.

The *UBI* is the recognition that every human being has value to the community; that there are as many ways to serve the community as there are people in that community; that while some contributions may be obscure, all are nonetheless valuable; and that each member of the community needs enough income for a basic level of sustenance in order to be a contributing member of the community.

The concept of a UBI is not new. Political thinkers have been bouncing the idea around by for over 200 years. In 1797, Thomas Paine published *Agrarian Justice* where he proposed that every man and woman in American be paid a one-time stipend of £15 (about $1800 in today's dollars) upon reaching 21-years of age. Paine reasoned that this would foster economic independence, *so crucial to the budding democracy* (Reich).[159]

About 50 years ago, a UBI was being considered by that raving liberal President Richard Nixon. As a key component of the War on Poverty, the base income for a family of four would have been set at $1,600, the equivalent of approximately $10,000 today. Nixon advisors Senator Daniel Moynihan and economist Milton Friedman supported the plan, with Friedman saying that *poverty simply meant you were short on cash – nothing more, nothing less.*[160] Nixon favored replacing welfare with a small federal income *on which the family itself could build* in a system where *outside earnings would be encouraged, not discouraged.*[161]

Some people argue that a *universal dividend* would undermine the work ethic. Peter Barnes, in *Capitalism 3.0*, offers this counterargument:

> *This might be true if the dividends were very high, but is unlikely to be true if they're kept at a modest level. Such dividends would supplement, but not replace, labor income. At the same time, they'd give people a little more freedom to take time off or to engage in uncompensated*

work at home or in their communities. Actually, a case can be made for slightly reducing the work ethic. With ever more jobs moving overseas, it's by no means certain we can keep all Americans employed. If some people choose to work less, that might be a good thing.[162]

I am proposing that everyone chooses to work less. In fact, I suggest that we need a new understanding of the work ethic itself. Over the course of human history, the work ethic has morphed from being of service to the community to being a means of acquiring personal wealth and status. It can still be the second without losing the first. But here's what needs to be understood – If work is important to me, it's also important to you. We all need to feel that we are contributing to the commonwealth. To assure that there is enough work to go around, my allotment of paid work is now 24 hours a week, the same as yours. The new work ethic includes the understanding that any work beyond that point is either unpaid and voluntary, or a bit aynrandish.

WE CAN THINK about a UBI as a ***robotics dividend*** that everyone is entitled to. What would be a good number for UBI? Why not base it on statistics the government keeps on the poverty level? A few pages back, we saw the poverty level was $11,880 for a household of one. A $990/month UBI for every adult American would exactly equal that. This amount is close to Andy Stern's proposal for $1000/mo. in *Raising the Floor*[163] and Charles Murray's proposal for $10,000/yr. in his latest work *In Our Hands*[164]. A married couple would receive $23,760, very close to the poverty level for a family of four. All the income mother and father receive from employment will help the family rise above the poverty level, giving the children a better shot at financial success in their future.

The UBI would be paid by the federal government to every adult in the U.S. It would guarantee that each citizen has the funds available for basic food, clothing, and shelter. (That would help keep the economy humming.) It could eliminate many federal and state programs that are now focused on those basic needs, allowing the individuals, on their own, to access goods and services in the open markets. Social Security could be reduced by the amount of the UBI, with the remainder then safely modified to individually-held accounts like IRA's, all that possible because the UBI provides an income floor.

Comparing anti-poverty measures

Minimum Wage

Earned Income Tax Credit

Unconditional Basic Income

Which of these mechanisms, or what combination of the three, will do the best job of combating poverty? Let's look at the impact of each on the labor supply/demand curves:

Minimum Wage	Earned Income Tax Credit	Unconditional Basic Income
Higher wages will encourage workers into the labor force.* Labor Supply **UP**	Higher incomes via the EITC will encourage workers into the labor force. Labor Supply **UP**	An income floor assures that every adult will have the wherewithal to purchase basic goods & services, and for some, eliminate the perceived need to work. Labor Supply **DOWN**

Minimum Wage	Earned Income Tax Credit	Unconditional Basic Income
Higher wages will accelerate the adoption of new technology and automation, eliminating the need for more workers. Labor Demand **DOWN**	The lower cost of labor will encourage employers to hire more workers, as they take advantage of what is, in effect, a subsidy. Labor Demand **UP**	With more consumer power in market, we can expect a growing demand for goods and services. Labor Demand **UP**

* Neel Kashkari, president of the Minneapolis Federal Reserve, had this comment for companies complaining about labor shortages in 2017: *If you're not raising wages, then it just sounds like whining.*[165]

One concern of the EITC is that it will slow the adoption of automation. This is spelled out in an article from Ryan Avent in the *Economist* titled *The Productivity Paradox*:

> the abundance of labour, and downward pressure on wages, reduces the incentive to invest in new labour-saving technologies. Until pressed, firms don't overhaul and automate their warehouse or swap out some wait staff for touchscreens. So productivity within sectors grows more slowly than it otherwise might. There are dynamic effects as well: when you don't deploy new technologies because labour is cheap, you don't get all the tweaks and knock-on innovations and accumulation of intangible capital that contributes to still more productivity growth down the road.[166]

Looking in the opposite direction, at an accelerated application of production automation, Matthew Yglesias writes in a *Vox* posting titled *The automation myth*:

But robots are never going to take all the jobs. The problem with trying to envision "a world without work" is that it asks us to envision an unrealistically large change.

The more likely outcome is a world with less work. And that's a world we should welcome rather than fear. It's a world in which we can make some policy decisions we want to make, rather than decisions we really don't want to make.[167]

Yglesias suggests several options for workers to reduce the number of hours worked, including retiring at an earlier age, taking more vacation and holiday time off, and extended leave for new parents. I would have like to have seen a shorter workweek among the options.

Ryan Avent states that if robots <u>did</u> take over ALL the jobs, everything from CEO to dog-walker, at least it would be clarifying. But in the meantime, minimum wages, employment credits and guaranteed incomes may all be employed to combat poverty and guarantee a minimum family income. They should be utilized in conjunction with the 24-hour workweek, with the stipulation that every worker is compensated the same amount for 24 hours of work as he had been making in 40. And the minimum income should be indexed to the rate of inflation so that we don't have the fits-and-starts we experience now with the lagging minimum wage. This is not an act of charity. It is recognition that each and every member of the community is a contributor in one way or another.

In the John Hope Bryant book, *How the Poor Can Save Capitalism*,[168] he describes poverty as more than just financial difficulties. He talks about the condition of hopelessness, where:

generational prosperity is held hostage to a stifling lack of opportunity, the poor are trapped in an airtight room of financial and economic ignorance, and in time, lower levels of hope and the stench of poverty are locked in.[169]

Bryant says that those in poverty are dealt a triple whammy of misfortune:

- No education regarding financial matters, and no role models to show the way to success. (Bryant sees this a *civil rights* issue for the poor.)
- No good jobs available, no opportunities to get ahead.
- No self-confidence, no self-esteem.

Bryant tells us that poverty is not a condition limited to those with low income. Some people can get by with very little money, others need much more. Regardless of a family's raw income, if they are living paycheck-to-paycheck, they can feel impoverished. Bryant calls it *teetering ... precariously perched on the precipice of financial ruin.*

While it is true, then, that neither minimum wage, EITC, UBI, nor any combination of the three will guarantee that a worker will not live in poverty, we can at least do a better job of giving every working class family a fighting chance.

Seeing so much poverty everywhere makes me think that God is not rich. He gives the appearance of it, but I suspect some financial difficulties.

--Victor Hugo, Les Miserables

CHAPTER 11

Managing the Change

CAPITALISM REWARDS the nimble company, for the competitive landscape is ever changing. Consumer tastes can change on a whim (often with the encouragement of the advertising industry). Competitors enter and leave the market. Supplier capabilities shift, along with changes in the abundance and scarcity of raw materials and components. Technological advances change production processes. Even financial availability can shift as different instruments gain and lose favor. The company that can shift gears and respond to changes quickly is better able to take advantage of the shifting landscape in a competitive environment.

Moving from the 40-hour to the 24-hour workweek <u>will</u> cause great disruption to the labor market, no doubt about it. But it need not be detrimental to the broader economy <u>if</u> companies react with nimbleness and equanimity instead of rigidity and bitterness.

Attracting the best workers

If all else were equal (all else will not be equal, as I'll explain later in this chapter), an enterprise would have to increase their headcount by 67% just to keep pace with their current level of production. The labor market will be tipped on its head, with a sudden increase in positions that need to be filled. Companies will need to compete for good workers.

When this situation occurred in the past, employers would turn to the addition of benefits to attract workers – health insurance, pensions, vacation, sick leave. As we know now, health insurance and pensions turned out to be budget-busters.

Pension plans somehow managed to be a bad idea for both employers and employees.

- Bad for employers because they had to fund defined benefits plans for retirees who, with modern medical care, refused to die at a reasonable age.
- Bad for employees who didn't stick around long enough to reach a vested position on their pensions.

So, with strong encouragement from the financial industry, 401(k) and 403(b) plans were born. Employees loved them because they owned these savings plans, and there was no need to stick around at a company where you didn't want to work just so they wouldn't lose a non-portable pension. Employers loved them because they were able to phase out of the defined benefit pension plans and spend less money matching funds to 401(k) plans than the amount they had needed to fund the defined pensions plans.

Employer health insurance plans are an interesting study in inefficiency. Widely sold by the insurance industry following WWII, they were effectively used as an incentive to attract workers. The more generous the plan, the greater the incentive. They offered family coverage which was important in the early years of the baby boom. Everybody loved them. Employers didn't mind because the cost of the plans was included in the total compensation package (and deducted from what would otherwise be part of the employee's salary). Employees got "free" medical care for the whole family, not thinking about the lost wages part. The medical industry had more business than ever. And of course, the insurance companies thrived. The only problem – there was no cost containment anywhere. That's not a good situation anytime, but <u>especially</u> in a for-profit environment. The insurance companies and the hospitals made lots of profits, and the doctor were paid generously. As we know now, this was unsustainable. With Obamacare (I use the name with gratitude, not derision), however imperfect, we now have a mechanism for everyone to purchase health insurance. The best thing that could happen at this time would be for all employers, large and small, to drop health insurance from their compensation packages. That would force everyone to participate in the ACA, and with that much larger pool of participants, the insurance carriers could effectively cover their risk and lower their prices.

Without medical insurance or pensions to attract workers, companies will try other spiffs. These may be as trivial as foosball tables in the break room, or as socially significant as extended family leave. Or they could try paying their employees more.

Production bonuses

Franklin Delano Roosevelt delivered a speech on May 24, 1937 titled *A Fair Day's Pay for a Fair Day's Work*[170]. The focus of his talk, naturally, was on the Fair Day's Pay part. And rightly so, given conditions in the labor market in those times. But the flip side of this equation is important too. We must acknowledge what constitutes a Fair Day's Work.

Fred C. Andersen, founder of the very successful Andersen Windows in Bayport, Minnesota, had an answer for that question. He employed a bonus plan where factory workers could earn up to 140% of their normal day's pay by working at a pace he and the worker considered 140% 'normal'. The bonus plan was extremely productive for decades. Working at a normal pace, a worker would earn 100% on his paycheck. If he speeded up his work by 20%, he'd take home 20% more. If he pushed his production all the way to 140%, he'd earn 40% more.

The production bonus was capped at 140%. That was as far as he could go. If a worker zoomed along at a 150 – 160 – 170% pace, he still would earn 140% on his paycheck. There was good reason for the cap on the bonus – working faster than 140% the normal pace would result in errors.

Empirical time studies of a simple pick-and-place task bore this out. Subjects were asked to sit at a workstation with a rotating disk. The disk had cavities around the perimeter which were to be filled with marbles from a bin in front of the subject. The subject's task was to reach into the bin with both hands, grab two marbles and place them in the cavities on the disk; then repeat the hand motions, keeping up with the pace of the machine.

The machine could be set to rotate at any speed. Slow speeds made the task of picking and placing the marbles very easy. Faster speeds began to feel more like work. And really fast speeds resulted in lots of errors – marbles flying everywhere! Through these tests with several subjects, a baseline was established for a 100% pace – a speed at which most of the workers could keep up for prolonged periods of time without feeling like they were dawdling, nor feel overly rushed.

As the rotation of the machine sped up, some subjects could go lightning-fast, never missing a marble. But for most, errors start to occur around 140% the baseline.

Andersen Windows discovered the wisdom of setting a 40% max on production bonuses some time ago. This was based on years of closely observed production work on a wide variety of manual factory jobs. Workers feeding and receiving parts from wood-working machines were expected to inspect the pieces of wood as they went along, and toss any rejects aside. The same for workers on assembly lines – if a subassembly looked wrong, it was to be pulled out of the production flow.

If workers went beyond that 140% pace, the inspection task was the first task to be sacrificed. Then other errors would start to happen – parts dropping on the floor and getting dinged up, for example. So as it turned out, after years of observation, 140% 'normal' speed seemed a good heuristic to follow.

Something interesting happens on many factory jobs after a worker has been assigned on the same task for a time: he makes improvements to the process, some of which can significantly speed up the cycle time. Let's go back to the test station with the rotating disk and the marbles. Were this a real job, and the worker paid by the number of marbles properly placed, he may discover that he can pick up two marbles in each hand at one time, cutting the back-and-forth motion of his hands in half. Then he may find that he can grab three marbles at a time. And before long, that worker is able to reach the 140% pace with ease.

Two things that can happen at that point: the worker can keep his mouth shut and enjoy his good fortune to be on a job where he can earn 140% of his wages on such an easy job, or he can report his discovery to his supervisor. If he does the first, he ends up with a real easy job. If he does the second, the whole company benefits from the increase in productivity. The worker is supposed to report his discovery.

Any process improvement that a worker comes up with belongs to Andersen's, not to the worker; just as patents awarded to a researcher working in a company R&D lab belong to the company, not to the individual scientist or engineer. The worker at Andersen's is supposed to report the improvement to his supervisor. If he does that, and it becomes part of the standard for the job, the worker receives a bonus tied to the value of the improvement. If he chooses to hide the improvement, thinking he'll take advantage of his new, leisurely-paced job; the new method will eventually be discovered by management and adopted into practice anyway. In this case, the worker who came up with the improved method receives squat for his discovery.

A fair day's work

Most of our jobs are not nearly as simple as a pick-and-place operation, and consequently, the pace of our work is not nearly so easy to measure. But we do have a pretty good idea as to what constitutes a *fair day's work*. We've all had the experience of going home after a particularly good day at work and feeling: *'Well – I earned my nickel today'*. And we've had the opposite thought after a day when it felt like we were just spinning our wheels, and didn't really get much done.

Let's think about this from the viewpoint of what some of us would consider the best of all possible careers – that of a professional athlete. Think about how we talk about the great athletes of our time. If we refer to a jock as "a natural", we say it with appreciation of his natural-born skills, but not necessarily with admiration. Admiration is reserved for the player with natural skills who nonetheless drives himself hard every day at practice to bring himself and his teammates to the very pinnacle of their game.

That internal drive should apply to workers in every walk of life. And while being a desk-jockey may feel quite pedestrian compared to being a real jockey, putting forth an honest day's effort is still an admirable trait. With personal computers in the office environment, and with hardware and software continually being upgraded, each worker is capable of being more productive as time goes on. But are we? Or do we spend part of the workday looking for flamingo lawn ornaments on the internet?

Work smarter, not harder is the refrain we often hear. But for the 24-hour workweek to work for everyone, employees must step up to the plate and deliver their fair share of labor to the organization. In exchange for receiving *a fair week's pay for a fair week's work,* each worker must strive to accomplish as much as possible in the new, shorter workweek. How much more productive? Why not use the 140% productivity heuristic as a target? 24/40 x 140% = 84%. Could some of us comfortably produce 84% as much in 24 hours as we previously produced in 40 hours a week? For some jobs, that would be easy. For others, a stretch.

With a 24-hour workweek, employees are going to find themselves closing the gap in the $P_{employer} > P_{employee}$ inequality. With that new-found power, comes responsibility. Increased productivity is something all workers should strive for because it results in economic growth. Growth that is needed to lift more and more people out of poverty.

It must, therefore, become socially unacceptable to slack-off on the job, to behave in a way Frederick Taylor referred to as *soldiering* (a term surely not PC today). *Rent seeking* on the job, if you will. W. Edwards Deming, stressed the importance of the worker's role in quality control, and he proposed the following as attitudes that should be adopted. Each employee should:

- Absorb and live the company's mission, goals, and operating philosophy
- Look toward the long-term good of the firm, not solely toward short-term gains for yourself; consider the needs of investors, customers, and vendors
- Show genuine concern for constant improvement of quality
- Know exactly what your job is and strive for improvement

- Not demand and create stultifying seniority and work rules
- Avoid adversarial and competitive behavior between and within shifts and departments or with management; act as a part of a team for the common good of all.[171]

When workers are being paid the same amount for 24 hours of work as they had been receiving for 40, they must do their best to be committed to the long-term success of their company and their boss, and to put forth an effort commensurate with that raise.

The role of labor unions and growth of the middle class

If we define the middle class as those households falling between 2/3 and 2X the median household income, then by definition, we have always had a middle class. But it is only quite recently that so many of us find ourselves in that category.

Prior to and throughout most of the industrial age, there were the aristocratic owners of larger farms and factories – the upper class. There were successful professionals and merchants in town – the middle class. And there were the laborers - the lower class.

Labor unions changed that. The unions were an off-shoot of merchant and labor guilds. They gained significance with the need to protect vulnerable factory workers from abusive bosses, and as time went on, these organizations became a force to be reckoned with. Proof of that can be found in this amazing statistic: 50 years ago, Detroit, with over 2 million residents, was the fourth largest city in America, and it had the highest per capita income of any city in the country! After 80 years of automation on the factory floor, and after four decades of outsourcing and offshoring in the auto industry, the influence of the UAW has waned. Detroit is now home to around 700,000, and is far, far from having the highest per capita income.[172]

The impact of the declining power of labor unions can be seen on the following graph:

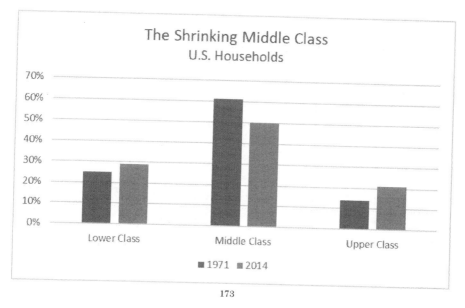

The Shrinking Middle Class
U.S. Households

(Lower Class, Middle Class, Upper Class — 1971, 2014)

173

Labor unions can become significant again, and help reverse this trend of a shrinking middle class. Unions, if they choose, can play a very positive role in the adoption of the shorter workweek. Labor leaders need to see the significant advantages of their members earning the same paycheck after three days of work that they had been earning in five. The unions need to acknowledge that there are no free rides, that all workers must 'pull their own weight', and they need to stop protecting slackers within their ranks. The unions should spend much more of their efforts on education and outreach.

Transitioning from weekend to workweek

With a 24-hour workweek, we will have to try to eliminate those *not-so-good* days at work. On average, our level of productivity/day should go up because we can be more focused on our jobs when on the job. Why is that? Because we now have two more days each week to take care of things at home: house work, doctors' appointments, school conferences, etc.

But with a longer weekend than workweek, workers must condition themselves to focus on their job quickly when they come in on Mondays (or whatever their first workday turns out to be). No slacking on Mondays when you only have Tuesday and Wednesday to make up the difference. I'm confident that workers will learn to adjust to their new schedules, just as their supervisors will.

Listen – if workers are given the gift of two extra days off every week, they will understand this has consequences. Children learning to ride bicycles figure this out very quickly. They know that for every exhilarating downhill coast, there is a corresponding work-for-it trudge uphill. (The longer weekend is meant to be the exhilarating downhill coast, in case anyone was not sure.)

There is some historical evidence that workers will respond with an attitude of more concentrated productivity. In 1973-74, there was great labor unrest in England. With coal miners out on strike and a growing energy crisis in the UK. Prime Minister Edward Health called for a 3-day workweek in all factories attempting to keep the whole economy from crashing. This experiment in energy austerity lasted just three months. Well after the fact, economists went back and measured the cost of this imposed trimmed-down workweek, and were amazed to find the overall effect on production was a drop of just 6%.[174]

Workforce participation

Several columns have appeared recently about the declining number of working-age men in the workforce, men neither employed nor seeking a job. The trend is contrary to the number of women in the workforce. The general implication is that these men are so discouraged by the lack of available jobs that they've given up looking for work.

I can think of another reason that is much less negative — they don't have to work! Remember the narrow definition of work we are using in this book: an economic activity where the employee supplies labor, his toil and time, in exchange for compensation from the employer. More and more, women are the ones with college degrees, and are holding down good fulltime jobs. They have become the primary breadwinners for the family. This enables more men to work less or to be stay-at-home dads, if they chose. With young children in the family, the high cost of daycare can take away the economic incentive to work. Why go to work in a $10-12 an hour job when you pay that much or more for daycare?

THAT SAID, there are some sad indications that some workers do not put forth *a fair day's labor for a fair day's pay*. One of those indicators can be seen in the substantial increase in claims for Social Security Disability Insurance. This has happened even though workplaces have become much safer (thanks to OSHA) and work overall has become less physical.

The quote below was pulled from a paper titled *The Growth in Social Security Disability Rolls: A Fiscal Crisis Unfolding* published by the National Bureau of Economic Research:

> *While aggregate population health has improved by most measures in recent decades, the rate of SSDI receipt among nonelderly adults has nearly doubled since 1984. We project that SSDI receipt will rise by an additional seventy percent before reaching a steady state rate of approximately 6.5 percent of adults between the ages of*

25 and 64, with cash benefit payments exceeding $150 billion annually (excluding Medicare).

We trace the rapid expansion of SSDI to: (1) congressional reforms to disability screening in 1984 that enabled workers with low mortality disorders such as back pain, arthritis and mental illness to more readily qualify for benefits; (2) a rise in the after-tax DI income replacement rate, which strengthened the incentives for workers to seek benefits; (3) and a rapid increase in female labor force participation that expanded the pool of insured workers. Notably, the aging of the baby boom generation has contributed little to the growth of SSDI to date.[175]

Some blame the increase in disability claims on the decrease in the overall general health of the workforce as we all become more sedentary and our diets less healthy. That may have something to do with it, but I'm afraid something else is involved here, something more insidious. It seems that in our culture, it is becoming more acceptable to *screw the company I work for because they've been screwing me for years.* And if this results with the government taking a hit, *screw them too.*

This attitude needs to change.

The 24-hour workweek should help. Adopting the shorter workweek should result in the balance-of-power in the employer/employee relationship swinging back toward the worker. And that should prove to be a major impetus to improve the attitude of workers 1) toward their job, 2) toward the community, and 3) toward personal responsibility. This alone would be a welcome cultural shift from where we are today.

With power, comes responsibility.

Inflation

Finally, we do need to take a look at the inflationary aspect of workers receiving the same compensation after 24 hours of work as they had been getting after 40 hours. That is a 67% raise. What will be the impact on inflation?

To answer that question, I turned to Louis Johnston, an economics professor at the College of St. Benedict and St. John's University. Dr. Johnston's response:

A 67% rise in wages would be a big one-time shock to the system. There would probably be much adjusting to be done, but it wouldn't have ongoing effects on prices, i.e., it wouldn't cause inflation. For example, inflation is currently around 2% per year. Under this plan you'd have a one-time bump of, say, 67%, but then inflation would return to 2%.

The adjustments firms would need to make are, to my mind, the bigger issue to think through.[176]

So where does the worker stand after his big raise and the corresponding one-time bump in inflation? If he does nothing new – if he keeps the same single fulltime job he had before – he will be no better nor worse off financially.

But he will have an additional 16 hours a week to call his own! He can choose to spend that time at home with the family, giving him the chance for a much richer lifestyle. Or he can opt to go back into the labor market for a second job. That <u>will</u> give him more buying power at the market.

I really appreciate Dr. Johnston's assessment, and agree wholeheartedly with his statement about the need for companies to be able to adjust to the new reality. And, as I wrote opening this chapter, *capitalism rewards the nimble company.*

CHAPTER 12

Positive Impact on Society and the Economy

THE TITLE OF THIS CHAPTER makes a very bold statement. Can a shorter workweek really have a positive impact on both society _and_ the economy? Can you really *have your cake, and time to eat it too?* I believe so. I believe the impact revolves around the benefits of more leisure time for all of us.

Let's start with the economic part. The Gross Domestic Product (GDP) is a measure of the economic output of a country. It is calculated:

$$GDP = Consumption + Government\ Expenditures$$
$$+\ Investment + Exports - Imports$$

When we divide a nation's GDP by the population, _GDP/capita_, it yields a pretty good measure of a country's well-being. A good measure, but not the measure. If it were the measure of well-being, then we should do everything in our power to make it higher. We should put children and seniors back to work.

Preposterous? Well, it wasn't that long ago that children entered the workforce as soon as they were able, and seniors remained in the workforce for as long as they were able. Children worked side-by-side with their parents throughout almost all recorded history. If we put them back to work now (and I'm not talking about just doing household chores or doing their homework), they could bring home a paycheck to support the family, just like mom and dad! Imagine the positive impact on the GDP.

And while we're at it, let's get all those able-bodied seniors back in the workforce. There's no reason why they should not be at work instead of spending their days golfing or fishing and sucking the nation's coffers dry with their social security and pension payments.

Well, we're not about to do that because we, as a society, have figured out that economic growth is not the only thing to be concerned about. We hold a special place in our hearts for children. We give them their own status legally. We bestow upon children the right to play and learn, and to be, insofar as possible, free from want and danger. At the other end of life, we have retirement. Through Social Security and pension plans, and with the encouragement of IRA's and the like, we've allowed people to retire from the workforce and still live in some comfort. We do this even though these retirement programs are expensive, especially now with so many retirees living into their 80's, 90's, and beyond.

In the interests of social cohesion and compassion, we take special care of our children and the elderly. We may grumble about paying our taxes and about inefficiencies in the programs, but we never question the central premise that this is the right thing to do.

Our social concern for children and the elderly is well-established. There's no reason why this concern should be limited to the young and the old. The well-being of working-age adults should be just as important to us. We do have economic programs to assist working-age adults who fall on hard times: AFDC, SNAP, Medicaid, etc. But we tend to grant this aid grudgingly (we have a tendency to blame the working poor for their own lot in life), especially in comparison of how open we are to support both children and seniors.

The pursuit of happiness

With agreement that the GDP is not the ultimate measure of a nation's progress, let's talk about the pursuit of happiness. The Sustainable Development Solutions Network, a panel of social scientists commissioned by the United Nations, conducts an annual survey measuring the level of happiness of citizens in countries all around the world.[177] The 2017 survey showed Norway as the happiest nation, followed closely by Denmark, Iceland, Switzerland, and Finland. At the other end of the scale, Burundi (154) and the Central African Republic (155) are, sadly, the least happy. The United States came in at No. 14 in the 2017 report.

The scholars found that three-quarters of the variability from one country to another can be explained by six measures:

- Gross domestic product per capita
- Healthy years of life expectancy
- Social support (having someone you can count on in times of trouble)
- Perceived freedom to make life choices
- Trust (as measured by perceived absence of corruption in government and business)
- Generosity (measured by charitable donations)

A nation can improve its standing on the overall happiness quotient by improving their score on any of these six measures.

It is interesting to compare the overall happiness scores of two countries, Japan and Sweden. Both are quite advanced economically, but they are two nations with very different attitudes about work. Japan is known for its culture of work. There is even a phenomenon known as *karoshi,* where some salaried workers have been known to literally work themselves to death. Sweden, on the other hand, has a reputation of a much more laid-back nation, where work is put in its place.

Despite these firmly held reputations, the difference in hours worked is not really that great, with the average hours worked per year in Japan 1713, and in Sweden 1621. Given that similarity, how are these two nations doing economically?

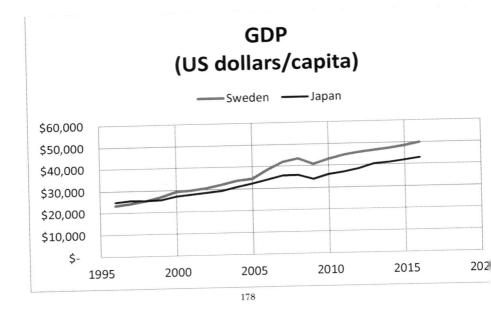

178

The chart above tracks GDP/capita over a twenty-year span. The two countries started at just about the same place in 1996, Japan at $24,830 and Sweden at $23,270. By 2016, Sweden had moved ahead to $49,930, 16% ahead of Japan at $42,850. And the happiness score of the two countries in 2016? Sweden ranked 10th from the top, Japan 51st.

Looking for a moment at the level of happiness here in the U.S., Dick Meyer of the Scripps Washington Bureau, closed a column on economic growth in the 20th century with the following:

> One aspect of 20th-century economic success has long puzzled social scientists: Americans received enormous increases in material benefits, prosperity and health, but did not report increased happiness and sense of well-being. It was just the opposite, in fact. Perhaps the key to flourishing amid ordinary times requires spiritual remedies more than material.[179]

Wrapping up this section, what is the moral of the story on happiness? We can prosper economically, and still have some fun doing it. We just need to learn again to let society drive our culture of work, not the other way around.

More leisure time

We all spend too much time at our place of employment, plain and simple. Working 24 hours a week instead of 40 will give all of us the chance to slow down and smell the roses. The chance to spend more time with our children, our parents, and our friends. The chance to volunteer more freely at the church or hospital, to offer time, talent, and treasure at the social service organization of our choice. The chance to take up hobbies that are personally fulfilling – not just smelling the roses – cultivating them, cutting them, arranging the blooms into bouquets; perhaps even grabbing paint brushes and canvas, and creating your own rendition of roses out in the warm sunshine of your garden.

There was an op-ed column by Laura Johnson titled *We all must make time for creativity in our lives.* Johnson writes about teaching art to a group of business executives, brought together to foster creativity on the job:

> *A team of corporate executive stares up at me. Behind the polish and power, I see the look of fear.*
>
> *I have witnessed this face of panic in many painting classes, but it's especially palpable in this group. I tell them again, kindly but firmly, to pick up their paintbrushes and begin painting the blank canvases... They insist that I explain exactly how to recreate the example painting—a colorful tree with flowers. It's a simple painting, designed to be finished in several hours, just for fun. Yet it seems to terrify them.*
>
> *These men and women make important business decisions every day. If I asked them to negotiate a multimillion-dollar deal, they wouldn't blink. Paint a tree? They balk.*
>
> *A week earlier, I taught the same painting to a Girl Scout troop, ages 9 to 11. I needed to race through my introduction, because they were so eager to start. Their eyes gazed longingly at the blank canvases, fingers twitching to grab brushes. Once they began, the girls asked me only for more paint colors. I saw wide trees, skinny trees, tall trees, short trees. None was the same, and not a single girl cared in the slightest.[180]*

Johnson asks:

> *When does this transition occur? At what point among e-mails, meetings, deadlines and long days do we forget the joy of creating?*

That question is best tackled in another work.

Art washes away from the soul the dust of everyday life. --Picasso

---

A white paper from the Oxford Martin School, published by Citigroup's Global Perspectives and Solutions, is titled: *Can Automation/Technology Reduce Working Hours Further and Increase Leisure Time Without Compromising the Standard of Living for All?*[181] In this paper, Andy Haldane from the Bank of England comments that work delivers more than money, that it creates a sense of personal worth and social attachment. Even so, people would enjoy more leisure time:

> *You never know: with time on our hands, we could actually start enjoying science, painting, writing and reading, leisure activities that were valued in the 1930's*

Normally, there are just two things that drive capitalist companies to invest in automation: the profit motive and a competitive market position. Never, it seems, do we take advantage of labor-saving devices by allowing everyone to work fewer hours. We should consider going there, and giving our workers free time to engage in activities of their own choosing.

Social pressure

How can we make the 24-hour workweek happen? With the political climate today, our lawmakers are much more interested in the well-being of the 'jobs creators' than the workers. Social pressure will have to be brought to bear to swing their attention to the employee half of the labor market. We care for our children. We care for our senior citizens. We should be just as willing to care for our 'working age' adults.

Employers in capitalist economies will not accept a shorter workweek without a fight. And to win this fight, workers will ultimately need both top-down and bottom-up strategies. Bottom-up pressure from labor and consumer movements. Top-down pressure from the state and national governments which foresee the need for change.

Ironically, the fight for a shorter workweek may be driven by consumers, not the workers. Labor unions are weak to non-existent in many countries. And unfortunately, many unions seem more interested in protecting the turf of current members (even ill-performing members) than expanding their reach to other workers.

Consumer boycotts have distinct advantages over labor strikes:

- they cannot be crushed by hired thugs or bussed-in scab-workers
- the government will have a hard time making consumer movements illegal

We have seen consumer boycotts have a tremendous impact on politics. Look back at how the racial segregation policy of apartheid was finally defeated in South Africa. Nelson Mandela, Archbishop Desmond Tutu and many others in South Africa brought attention to the injustices of apartheid to a worldwide audience. And it was consumers who responded to the injustice and put pressure on international companies to pull out of the South Africa. When the multinationals abandoned South Africa en masse, it had a significant impact on the economy of the country, and then even South African companies pressed the government to capitulate. Along with relentless pressure from

Mandela and his companions, this eventually was enough to break the will of the South African government, and thankfully send the policy of apartheid into the historic dustbin.

Shoppers are generally more interested in getting bargains than in the labor provenance of the products they buy. But consumers are not without a conscience. Consider the impact of consumer movements on the sale of cage-free eggs and shade-grown coffee. The driver behind the first – a more humane treatment of chickens, and the second – a more sustainable method of growing coffee.

With social media at our disposal, there is every reason to believe consumers could be just as influential in instituting a more humane treatment of workers. Specifically, consumers could choose to buy only shirts with a 24HR label attached.

An optimistic conclusion

Automobiles will not earn the right to be called AUTOmobiles until they learn to drive themselves. Fortunately, several forward-thinking high-tech and automotive companies are teaming up to develop driverless cars as we speak. When self-driving cars become widely available, they will be wonderful tools for all of us, especially the elderly. Sooner or later, we will all reach the age of diminished driving ability (my wife thinks I'm already there). Seniors will be able to maintain their mobility and their independence for much longer with a self-driving car. This will be highly beneficial to our quality of life, and allow us to stay active in the consumer marketplace for much longer. This will be good for the GDP, but not so good for certain segments of the labor market. Namely, those workers who now drive to earn a living.

Even with that loss of jobs, an optimist will look at the bright side. I don't think any will argue that we won't be better off collectively with safe, clean, and eventually affordable AUTOmobiles at our disposal.

AN OPTIMIST knows that we always do manage to find a way to deal with life's hardest questions. Every so often, there are stories in the paper about the decisions we face regarding end-of-life health care. In an excellent column titled *How much should be done to save a life?*, Dr. Eric Snoey tells us about his relationship with a 90-year-old patient who was admitted to the emergency room struggling mightily to breathe. With a weak heart and failing kidneys, her lungs had filled up with fluid, and every gasping breath was a mixture of water and air. She was, in effect, drowning.

Standard operating procedure in these cases is intubation; but months earlier the patient had completed an Advance Directive – no intubation, no chest compressions, no invasive procedures. As the senior doctor on duty, it was Dr. Snoey's decision what to do next. Living will or not, this is never an easy call. He writes: *In truth, the options aren't black and white but intensely gray, defined by nuance and competing goals, and in the moment, doctor and patient may struggle to find common ground.*

In this case, the patient made her wishes clear. In addition to her Advance Directive, she struggled to get these words out for the doctor: *"This ... is the end ... of my life."* It wasn't a question. It was a statement. Even with all this clear guidance, Dr. Snoey tells us it's still not easy to let a patient die when there's more that can be done, and as he called for *"supportive care only"*, it was *an uncomfortable, conflicted moment for everyone in the room.* [182]

Doctors have machines and drugs that can keep bodies alive virtually forever (if having a pulse is considered alive). But should they? Should not the quality of one's life be factored into the equation? Does it make sense to extend life when life itself has become miserably unbearable? This ability to extend life at all costs raises some of those REALLY BIG questions that society must deal with sooner or later.

While *end-of-work* questions should not rise to the level of importance as those that deal with *end-of-life*, they are, nonetheless, REALLY BIG questions. Questions that we, as a society, will eventually have to deal with.

But not yet.

New occupations are still being born as old jobs fade away. Just not as many. And not as fast. The 24-hour workweek is not a permanent answer to the question of work. But I believe it is a pretty good stop-gap measure that will have the desired impacts of increasing labor demand while dropping unemployment rates, and in the process give each worker a little more bargaining power. It should also have a long-term positive impact on the global economy.

I HAVE NO ILLUSIONS that my proposal will be accepted as is, or without a fight. But this is a good place to open the discussion on a shorter standard workweek. Will we figure it out? Yes, I believe we will. And I say that with the confidence of an optimist.

An optimist knows that the worldwide literacy rate has risen from less than half to over 85% in the last 50 years, and in just the last two decades, both the worldwide infant mortality rate and the number of people living in extreme poverty have dropped in half.[183] Economic progress has us all headed in the right direction.

An optimist believes that people are at least as smart as ducks:

> *Line up four ducks in a row on a single log at nap time. There's a very good chance that the two ducks in the middle will sleep with both eyes closed, regenerating both hemispheres of the brain in their slumber. But the duck on the right will keep his right eye open, and the duck on the left will keep his left eye open. These "on guard" ducks can sleep with half of their brain at a time, keeping the other half of the brain alert, aware of what's going on outside their head. They do this to protect both themselves AND the other three napping ducks from dangerous predators.*

If ducks are smart enough to figure out how to look out for each other and nap safely; human beings, with 2 million years of genetic predisposition to be socially cooperative animals, will surely figure out how to protect each other from unscrupulous capitalist predators. You know – the ones ordering foie gras for lunch.

ENDNOTES

Chapter 1
[1] Wilson, Edward O., *The Social Conquest of Earth*, (Liveright Publishing Corporation, 2012).
[2] *Ibid*, p. 129.
[3] *Ibid*, p. 243.
[4] *Ibid*, p. 273.
[5] *Ibid*, p. 289.
[6] Natural History Museum, London, www.nhm.ac.uk
[7] Applebaum, Herbert, *The Concept of Work*, (SUNY Press, 1992).
[8] *Ibid*, p. xii.
[9] Applebaum, p. 193.
[10] *Ibid*, p. 192.
[11] *Ibid*, p. 195.
[12] *Ibid*, p. 322.
[13] *Ibid*, p. 325.
[14] Donkin, Richard, *Blood Sweat & Tears*, (Texere LLC, 2001), p. 110.
[15] http://www.history.com/topics/martin-luther-and-the-95-theses
[16] Donkin, p. 242.

Chapter 2
[17] US Department of Labor, 2012 Occupational Employment Statistics.
[18] Disraeli, Benjamin, *Sybil, or The Two Nations*, 1845, (Kindle), Book 3 Chapter 8
[19] Samuelson, Robert, *A new era of labor scarcity?*, (Pioneer Press [from Washington Post], 9/5/16)
[20] Donkin, p. 215.
[21] Farrell, Chris, *Unretirement*, (Bloomsbury Press, 2014), ch 9 [kindle 58%]
[22] Farrell, *Working longer may benefit your health*, (StarTribune [NY Times], 3/12/17)
[23] Ton, Zeynep, *The Good Jobs Strategy*, (Lake Union Publishing, 2014), Ch. 7
[24] Lindgren, Amy, *A personal perspective on workplace scheduling*, (Pioneer Press, 10/11/15)
[25] http://wikipedia.org/wiki/job-characteristc-theory
[26] Davidson, Adam, *Managed by Q's 'Good Jobs' Gamble*, (New York Times Magazine, 2/28/16)
[27] *Ibid*
[28] Schwartz, Barry, *Rethinking Work*, (NY Times, 8/30/15)
[29] Barlow, Elizabeth, *The New York Magazine Environmental Teach-In*, (New York Magazine, 3/30/70), p. 30.

[30] Borjas, George J., *Labor Economics*, Sixth Edition, (McGraw-Hill, 2013), p 506.

[31] Mullainathan, Sendhil and Shafir, Eldar, *Scarcity, Why Having Too Little Matters So Much*, (Times Books, Henry Holt and Company, 2013), p. 155.

[32] Barreca, Gina, *Take it from teacher: Johnny needs a job*, (Pioneer Press, 8/17/15)

[33] Avent, Ryan, *The Wealth of Humans*, (St. Martin's Press, 2017), Kindle Loc 220.

[34] Florida, Richard, *The Rise of the Creative Class Revisted*, (Basic Books, 2012)

[35] Brooks, David, *Bobos in Paradise* (Simon & Schuster, 2000)

[36] Ehrenreich, Barbara, *Nickel and Dimed*, (Picador, 2011)

[37] Shipler, David, *The Working Poor*, (Vintage, 2005)

Chapter 3

[38] Thoreau, Henry David, *Walden, or, Life in the Woods,* 1854 (Kindle, *The Complete Novels*), loc. 20510 of 94876.

[39] Schafer, Lee, *Cleese makes the case for creativity*, (StarTribune, 2/17/16)

[40] http://www.econlib.org/library/Essays/rdPncl1.html

[41] *Earth, Composition and Structure*, (Wikipedia, 2016)

[42] https://clipartxtras.com

[43] De Graaf, John; Wann, David; and Naylor, Thomas; *Affluenza*, (Berrett-Koehler Publishers, Inc., 2001)

[44] Barber, Benjamin, *Consumed*, (W. W. Norton & Co, 2007)

[45] Luttwak, Edward, *Turbo-Capitalism*, (Weidenfeld & Nicolson, 1998)

[46] Kunstler, James, *The Geography of Nowhere*, (Simon & Schuster, 1993)

[47] Will, George, *Starbucks and our pursuit of snobbery*, (Pioneer Press [from Washington Post], 12/16/16)

Chapter 4

[48] Borjas, p. 21.

[49] Hunnicutt, Benjamin, *Free Time*, (Temple University Press, 2013), p. 2.

[50] *Ibid,* p. 1.

[51] *Ibid,* p. 109.

[52] *Ibid,* p. 117.

[53] *Ibid,* p. 118.

[54] http://www.epi.org/pay-agenda/

[55] Frey, Holmes, Osborne, *Technology at Work v2.0*, (Oxford Martin School/Citi GPS, Jan 2016)

[56] Bailey, James, Washington Post, *Take some time off – for yourself and others* (StarTribune, 7/3/16)

[57] http://www.projecttimeoff.com/issue

[58] McReynolds, Ginny, Washington Post, *No longer slaves to the clock*, (Pioneer Press, 6/28/16)

[59] Farrell, Chris, *Unretirement*, (Bloomsbury Press, 2014)

[60] Amram, Fred M.B., *There's no reason to mock the beanbag chair*, (StarTribune, 1/28/16)
[61] http://read.gov/aesop/052.html

Chapter 5
[62] Rifkin, Jeremy, *The End of Work*, (Tharcher/Putnam, 1995)
[63] Ford, Martin, *The Lights in the Tunnel*, (Acculant Publishing, 2009)
[64] Brynjolfsson, Erik and McAfee, Andrew, *Race Against the Machine*, (Digital Frontier Press, 2011)
[65] Kaplan, Jerry, *Artificial Intelligence, what everyone needs to know*, (Oxford Univ. Press, 2016)
[66] Manyika, James, *Technology, jobs, and the future of work*, (McKinsey Global Institute, Dec 2016)
[67] www.forrester.com/Robots+AI+Will+Replace+7+Of+US+Jobs+By+2025/-/E-PRE9246
[68] Cotter, Michael, *The Killdeer, And Other Stories From the Farming Life*, (Parkhurst Brothers, 2014)
[69] Cotter, Michael, *Growing Up On A Minnesota Farm*, (Arcadia Publishing, 2001), p. 48.
[70] *Ibid*, p. 57.
[71] Rochford, Harold, (Mower County Historical Society), Photo 93.609.0320, Threshing Scene, file 503 page 4.
[72] www.sourcewatch.org/index.php/coal
[73] Reich, Robert, *Truths about free trade*, (Pioneer Press, 3/17/16)
[74] Gordon, Robert J., *The Rise and Fall of American Growth*, (Princeton University Press, 2016), p. 499.
[75] Reich, Robert, *Saving Capitalism*, (Alfred A. Knoff, 2015), p. 206.
[76] Rugaber, Christopher (Associated Press), *The great divide*, (Pioneer Press, 7/10/16)
[77] Avent, Ryan, *The Wealth of Humans*, (St. Martin's Press, 2016), Kindle Ch 8, loc. 2856.
[78] Bertoni, Robert, shared correspondence, March 2016.
[79] Popper, Nathaniel, *The Robots Are Coming for Wall Street*, (New York Times Magazine, 2/28/16)
[80] Goel, Ashok, http://www.news.gatech.edu/2016/05/09/artificial-intelligence-course-creates-ai-teaching-assistant
[81] Avent, Ryan, *The Wealth of Humans*, (St. Martin's Press, 2016), Kindle Ch 2, loc. 762-771.

Chapter 6
[82] http://www.msf.org/en/msf-charter-and-principles
[83] Diamond, Jared, *Guns, Germs, and Steel* (get publisher, etc.)
[84] Bregman, Rutger, *Utopia for Realists*, (The Correspondent, 2016)

[85] Davidson, Adam, *Voters Left And Right Are Anti-Free Trade* (NPR News, 3/13/16).

[86] Tice, D.J., *Antiglobalism: A bipartisan affliction*, (Star Tribune, 8/7/16)

[87] Oppenheimer, Andres, *Hoover, not Hitler, is the apt comparison for Trump*, (Pioneer Press, 3/13/16)

[88] *Toyota to boost Indiana factory*, (Pioneer Press, 1/25/17)

[89] http://www.gallup.com/poll/166211/worldwide-median-household-income-000.aspx

[90] Ryssdal, Kai, *In today's economy, even two-income families suffer...*, (Marketplace, PBS NewsHour, 6/10/16)

[91] De Sam Lazaro, Fred, *Dusty mining conditions...*, (Untold Stories, PBS NewsHour, 4/7/16)

[92] Perry, Mark, *Experts agree: Free trade is good*, (Pioneer Press, 3/22/16)

[93] Boak, Josh and Swanson, Emily, *Poll: Americans prefer low prices to 'Made in USA' items*, (Associated Press, 4/15/16)

[94] Will, George, *Whirlpool has Washington in a spin cycle*, (Washington Post, Pioneer Press, 12/17/17)

[95] Cahuc, Carcillo, & Zylberberg, *Labor Economics*, (MIT Press, 2014), pp. xvii-xx.

[96] Kasperkevic, Jana, *Immigrants around the world* (NPR Marketplace, 6/15/17)

[97] Frankel, Todd, *Foxconn's broken pledges cast doubt on Trump's plan for jobs*, (StarTribune [from Washington Post], 3/6/17)

Chapter 7

[98] Serling, Rod, *The Lateness of the Hour*, (Twilight Zone, 12/2/60)

[99] Tingley, Kim, *Learning to Love our Robot Co-workers*, (NY Times Mag., 2/23/17)

[100] https://en.wikipedia.org/wiki/Symphony_No._5_(Beethoven)

[101] Bregman, Rutger, *Utopia for Realists*, (The Correspondent, 2016), Ch.8.

[102] Grant, Tracy, *How caring for a dying husband made life worth living*, (PBS Newhour, 9/27/16)

[103] Stowe, Harriet Beecher, *Uncle Tom's Cabin*, (Kindle edition), Chapter XV

[104] Applebaum, Binyamin, *The Jobs Americans Do*, (NY Times Magazine, 2/23/17)

[105] https://www.bls.gov/oes/current/oes_nat.htm#00-0000

[106] Meyer, Dick, *The plague of the white working class*, (Scripps Wash. Bur., StarTribune, 4/9/17)

Chapter 8

[107] Avent, Ryan, *The Wealth of Humans*, (St. Martin's Press, 2016), Kindle Loc 1526.

[108] Reich, Robert, *In contrast to no-lose socialism*, (Pioneer Press, 5/6/16)

[109] *Ibid*

[110] Hallock, Kevin, *Pay*, (Cambridge University Press, 2012)

[111] Schuman, Michael, *Forget $15 minimum wage. What about bonuses?* (Pioneer Press, 9/21/16)

[112] Avent, Ryan, *The Wealth of Humans*, (St. Martin's Press, 2016), Ch. 5, Kindle loc. 1586.

[113] Reich, *Saving Capitalism,* p. 98.

[114] Hanauer, Nick, *The Pitchforks are Coming … For Us Plutocrats,* (Politico Magazine, June/August 2014)

[115] Belz, Adam, *Low-wage jobs worth a bit more*, (StarTribune, 3/22/16)

[116] http://www.epi.org/publication/charting-wage-stagnation/

[117] Reich, *Saving Capitalism*, p. 137.

[118] Gordon, p. 613.

[119] http://www.epi.org/publication/charting-wage-stagnation/

[120] Manyika, James, *Technology, jobs, and the future of work*, (McKinsey Global Institute, Dec 2016)

[121] Reich, *Saving Capitalism*, p. 61.

Chapter 9

[122] Piketty, Thomas, *Capital in the Twenty-first Century* (The Belknap Press, 2014), p. 571.

[123] Korten, David C., *The Post-Corporate World*, (Berrett-Koehler Publishers, 1999), p. 37.

[124] Reich, *Saving Capitalism*, p. 45.

[125] *Ibid*, p. 38.

[126] Meyerson, Harold, *Fed forgets who has the power (hint: not workers)*, (StarTribune, 12/19/15)

[127] Mukunda, Gautam, *What Bernie Sanders and Donald Trump get wrong about Wall Street*, (Pioneer Press [from Washington Post], 4/28/16)

[128] Branswell, Helen, *Big pharmaceutical companies reluctant to produce Zika vaccine*, (PBS Newshour, The Rundown, 8/9/16)

[129] Avent, Ryan, *The Wealth of Humans*, (St. Martin's Press, 2016), Ch. 6, Kindle loc. 1985, 1994.

[130] Tcherneva, Pavlina, *When a Rising Tide Sinks Most Boats*, (Levy Economics Institute of Bard College, Policy Note 2015/4)

[131] Smith, Noah, *Hey you in a nation of ruts and inequality: Guess what?*, (Star Tribune, 11/13/16)

[132] Young, Stephen, *The realignment of the working class*, (StarTribune, 9/17/16)

[133] Bregman, Ch. 9.

[134] Zucman, Gabriel, *The Hidden Wealth of Nations*, (The University of Chicago Press, 2015)

[135] New York Times, *Ireland's GDP gets big boost from 'magic' of inversion deals*, (Star Tribune, 7/13/16)

[136] Kanter and Scott, NY Times, *E.U. orders Apple to repay $14.5B in taxes to Ireland*, (StarTribune, 8/31/16)

[137] http://www.cauxroundtable.org/index.cfm?menuid=8

[138] Madland, David and Walter, Karla, *Growing the Wealth*, (Center for American Progress, April 2013)

[139] Gates, Jeff, *The Ownership Solution*, (Perseus Books, 1998)

[140] *Ibid*, p. xx.

[141] http://www.cauxroundtable.org/index.cfm?menuid=8

[142] McKay, Harvey, *How to keep employees working for you*, (StarTribune, 4/3/17)

[143] Humprey, Hubert H, *Letter to Editor*, (Washington Post, 7/20/1976)

Chapter 10

[144] Hamermesh, Daniel, *Workdays, Workhours and Work Schedules*, (W.E. Upjohn Institute for Employment Research, 1996), p. 131.

[145] https://en.wikipedia.org/wiki/Adolf_Meyer_(psychiatrist)

[146] Bregman, Ch. 7.

[147] Borjas, George J., *Labor Economics*, Sixth Edition, (McGraw-Hill, 2013)

[148] Alderman, Liz, *In Sweden, Happiness in a Shorter Workday Can't Overcome the Cost*, (NY Times, 1/6/17)

[149] Young, Stephan, *Moral Capitalism*, (Berrett-Koehler Publishers, 2003), p. 56.

[150] Reich, *Saving Capitalism*, p. 81.

[151] Reich, Robert, *Saving Capitalism For the Many, Not the Few*, (Borzoi Book, 2015), p. 5.

[152] *Ibid,* p. 84.

[153] Banaian, King, *Let workers speak for themselves*, (Pioneer Press, 6-30/16)

[154] Stowe, Chapter XIX.

[155] Donkin, p. 21.

[156] Marty, John, *$15 an hour – first Minneapolis, then statewide* (StarTribune, 6/29/16)

[157] http://www.irp.wisc.edu/faqs/faq2.htm

[158] https://aspe.hhs.gov/poverty-guidelines

[159] Reich, *Saving Capitalism*, p. 216.

[160] Bregman, Ch. 6.

[161] StarTribune editorial, *Clinton's smart plan to help fight poverty*, (StarTribune, 10/14/16)

[162] Barnes, Peter, *Capitalism 3.0*, (Berrett-Koehler Publishers, 2006), p. 116

[163] Stern, Andy, *Raising the Floor*, (PublicAffairs, 2016)

[164] Murray, Charles, *In Our Hands*, (AEI Press, 2006)

[165] Lotterman, Edward, *Target's wage move reflects market realities*, (Pioneer Press, 10/1/17)

[166] Avent, Ryan, *The Productivity Paradox*, (Medium [The Economist], 3/16/17)

[167] Yglesias, Matthew, *The automation myth*, (Vox, 7/27/15)

[168] Bryant, John Hope, *How the Poor Can Save Capitalism*, (Berret-Koehler Publishers, 2014)

[169] *Ibid*, p. 76.

Chapter 11

[170] Roosevelt, Franklin Delano, *A Fair Day's Pay for a Fair Day's Work*, (speech delivered 5/24/1937)

[171] Young, p. 112.

[172] Bryant, p.17.

[173] Pioneer Press, *The Great Divide*, (6/10/16)

[174] http://www.shorterworkweek.com/econeffect.html

[175] Autor, David and Duggan, Mark, *The Growth in Social Security Disability Rolls: A Fiscal Crisis Unfolding*, (NBER Working Paper No. 12436, August 2006)

Chapter 12

[176] Johnston, Louis, shared correspondence, Oct 2016

[177] http://worldhappiness.report/ed/2017/

[178] https://data.oecd.org/natincome/gross-national-income.htm#indicator-chart

[179] Meyer, Dick, *The best of times are in the rearview mirror*, (StarTribune, 2/14/16)

[180] Johnson, Laura M., *We all must make time for creativity in our lives*, (StarTribune, 9/15/16)

[181] Frey, Osborne, Holmes, *Technology at Work v2.0*, (Oxford Martin School/CitiGPS, Jan 2016)

[182] Snoey, Eric, *How much should be done to save a life?* (Pioneer Press [from Los Angeles Times], 5/29/16)

[183] Kristof, Nicholas, *The best news you don't know*, (Pioneer Press [from NY Times], 9/29/16)